DOUGLAS SIRK

PHILOSOPHICAL FILMMAKERS

Series editor: Costica Bradatan is a Professor of Humanities at Texas Tech University, USA, and an Honorary Research Professor of Philosophy at the University of Queensland, Australia. He is the author of *Dying for Ideas: The Dangerous Lives of the Philosophers* (Bloomsbury, 2015), among other books.

Films can ask big questions about human existence: what it means to be alive, to be afraid, to be moral, to be loved. The *Philosophical Filmmakers* series examines the work of influential directors, through the writing of thinkers wanting to grapple with the rocky territory where film and philosophy touch borders.

Each book involves a philosopher engaging with an individual filmmaker's work, revealing how it has inspired the author's own philosophical perspectives and how critical engagement with those films can expand our intellectual horizons.

Other titles in the series:

Eric Rohmer, Vittorio Hösle
Werner Herzog, Richard Eldridge
Terrence Malick, Robert Sinnerbrink
Kenneth Lonergan, Todd May
Shyam Benegal, Samir Chopra

Other titles forthcoming:

Christopher Nolan, Robbie Goh
Leni Riefenstahl, Jakob Lothe

DOUGLAS SIRK

Filmmaker and Philosopher

ROBERT B. PIPPIN

BLOOMSBURY ACADEMIC
LONDON • NEW YORK • OXFORD • NEW DELHI • SYDNEY

BLOOMSBURY ACADEMIC
Bloomsbury Publishing Plc
50 Bedford Square, London, WC1B 3DP, UK
1385 Broadway, New York, NY 10018, USA
29 Earlsfort Terrace, Dublin 2, Ireland

BLOOMSBURY, BLOOMSBURY ACADEMIC and the Diana logo are trademarks of
Bloomsbury Publishing Plc

First published in Great Britain 2021

Library of Congress Cataloging-in-Publication Data
Names: Pippin, Robert B., 1948– author.
Title: Douglas Sirk : filmmaker and philosopher / Robert B. Pippin.
Description: New York : Bloomsbury Academic, 2021. | Series: Philosophical filmmakers |
Includes bibliographical references and index. |
Identifiers: LCCN 2020049931 (print) | LCCN 2020049932 (ebook) |
ISBN 9781350195660 (hardback) | ISBN 9781350195677 (paperback) |
ISBN 9781350195684 (ebook) | ISBN 9781350195691 (epub)
Subjects: LCSH: Sirk, Douglas, 1897–1987–Criticism and interpretation. | Melodrama in
motion pictures. | Irony in motion pictures. | Philosophy in motion pictures. |
Motion pictures–United States–History–20th century. | Motion picture producers and
directors–United States–Biography. | Motion picture producers
and directors–Germany–Biography.
Classification: LCC PN1998.3.S57 P57 2021 (print) | LCC PN1998.3.S57 (ebook) |
DDC 791.4302/33092 [B]—dc23
LC record available at https://lccn.loc.gov/2020049931
LC ebook record available at https://lccn.loc.gov/2020049932

ISBN: HB   978-1-3501-9566-0
        PB: 978-1-3501-9567-7
        ePDF: 978-1-3501-9568-4
        eBook: 978-1-3501-9569-1

Series: Philosophical Filmmakers

Typeset by RefineCatch Limited, Bungay, Suffolk
Printed and bound by CPI Group (UK) Ltd, Croydon, CR0 4YY

To find out more about our authors and books visit www.bloomsbury.com
and sign up for our newsletters.

CONTENTS

ACKNOWLEDGEMENTS

An earlier, different form of Chapter Two originally appeared in *Critical Inquiry* (vol. 45; Summer 2019) and I am grateful to the editors for allowing me to retain copyright. Many thanks to Amy Levine for preparing the index. I am also very grateful for comments provided by and for conversations with Fred Rush, Dan Morgan, Richard Neer, Tom Gunning, Francey Russell and Michael Fried. I am especially indebted to Mark Wilson.

1

Introduction:
Irony as Subversion

The characteristics we associate with film melodrama, a form traditionally taken to be a demotic or 'low art' form, are feverishly intense suffering, overwhelmingly of women,[1] expressed around a great emotional crisis, usually involving romantic and/or familial love. In many stock melodramas there are clearly identifiable villains and victims, but in many others, like those by Douglas Sirk that will be discussed in this book, there are not. That is, the suffering is caused not by villains but by those who love each other. This is all presented in a cinematic style in which such crises are given expression in a way that seems to many viewers hyperbolic, excessive, overwrought, obvious (particularly in the musical score), something that usually prompts complaints about simplification and manipulation. When we point to such excess, we mean that the expression of emotion in

---

[1]Predominantly but not exclusively. According to Laura Mulvey, *Written on the Wind* and *Tarnished Angels* stand out because of their treatment of male victims of patriarchal families in capitalism; see Laura Mulvey, 'Notes on Sirk and Melodrama', in *Home Is Where the Heart Is*, ed. Christine Gledhill (London, 1994), pp. 76–77.

film melodrama goes beyond what we find 'appropriate'. 'Don't be so melodramatic!' almost always has the same practical force as 'You are over-reacting', and we often mean to imply neurosis, childishness, self-indulgence. In the simplest sense this excess in movies embarrasses us. In Sirk's films, this heightened emotionality is expressed by an unusually intense, bright colour palette in sets and clothes (and so are characterized as anti-illusionistic), sometimes almost garish lighting, hyper-sharp, deep focus, frequent close-ups of such expressivity, a lush, romantic and quite unsubtle sound track, and, at the very least, ambiguous happy endings.

Modern melodramas in novels and dramas, considered as a narrative style, or, as Peter Brooks has argued, 'an imaginative mode', and an 'inescapable dimension of modern consciousness',[2] have a historical origin too. In the late eighteenth century, more and more small local theatres in France proliferated in and beyond Paris, and the French court began to lose their hitherto strict control of permissible theatrical content. Tragedy as the dominant dramatic genre began to be displaced by a new genre. The term 'melodrama' was apparently coined by Rousseau to describe his dramas accompanied by music, and he is sometimes given credit for the first modern melodrama, his *Pygmalion*, written in 1762 and staged for the first time in Lyon in 1770. By the nineteenth century the genre was well established and

---

[2]Peter Brooks, *The Melodramatic Imagination: Balzac, Henry James, Melodrama and the Mode of Excess* (New Haven: Yale University Press, 1976), p. vii. Thomas Elsaesser, in probably the single most influential film studies article on melodrama, 'Tales of Sound and Fury: Observations on the Family Melodrama', first published in *Monogram* in 1972, and reprinted in *Home is Where the Heart Is*, summarizes a discussion of melodrama as 'a form which carried its own values and already embodied its own significant content; it served as the literary equivalent of a particular, historical and socially conditioned mode of experience', p. 49.

from 1800 to 1830 the most popular dramatist in France was Guilbert de Pixerécourt, and his plays were clearly recognizable as melodramas. In terms of plot, a typical melodrama described the suffering of women; very frequently a working-class or middle-class young woman or girl subject to unwanted attention by an aristocrat, who eventually forced himself on the girl, after threatening to destroy her entire family financially. Often a pregnancy and a suicide would then ensue; sometimes a last minute rescue by an admiring young man from the village. Another typical plot depicts some great sacrifice required of a woman, as in films like *Stella Dallas*, *Now, Voyager* and *Letter from an Unknown Woman*. But there were many different such plots, full of clear and often simplistic differentiation between good and evil characters, undeserved suffering, and an intense emotional tone very obviously aimed at provoking pity, outrage and tears from the audience. Most importantly, while in classical and neo-classical tragedies, heroic characters were extraordinary people, usually aristocratic rulers on whom the fate of the nation depended, and who represented vast ethical and historical forces like the family, the city, the divine, fate, most melodramas concerned ordinary bourgeois commoners. This was a reflection of the view of democratic egalitarianism.[3] There are no such superior beings; everyone is subject to the same joys and indignities of ordinary life. And there were no such historical or universal forces at stake, much happened by blind chance, and if a victim was saved at the last possible moment by some *deus ex machina* intervention, it meant nothing beyond the contingent frame of the play, a mere happy ending. Melodramas could thus be said to begin the

---

[3]See Brooks, *The Melodramatic Imagination*, p. 15.

exploration of human self-understanding in a disenchanted, secular world (this is Brooks's view), as well as raising the question of whether great art that could rival past masterpieces could be made within and about such an ordinary world. (In film melodrama, it is often the use of cinematic and musical means to suggest the enormous significance of the ordinary that risks the ridiculous, an almost comically exaggerated significance that is more than the ordinary can bear.) Or characters over-invest so much and so desperately in romantic and familial love because of the ever more apparent banality, repetitiveness and enormous pressure for conformism in the new form of capitalist life. The excess is not merely a formal feature of the art form, but an expression of a form of desperation, and the theatrical, public expression of such emotions is a sign of the futility of such feeling; they have no other 'outlet'. (If we are now largely unresponsive, it may not be because we are cooler or hipper, but because such desperate resistance has gone dead; the intense yearning has been co-opted. Perhaps that is the mark of being cooler and hipper.) One possible explanation for the excess and hysteria could stem from characters expecting far too much of romantic and familial love, the only arenas available for any individual expressiveness genuinely one's own, even if inevitably disappointed. That inevitable disappointment is our theme below, but again, Sirk's apparent pessimism about friendship and love is deeply historical and locally inflected, as any interrogation of friendship and love should be. It was in the American world of the 1950s, the world of a market economy and the system of wage labour, the nuclear family, romantic love and eventually mass-consumer societies, where such failure might be expected. The ordinary familial and romantic dramas of life were the subjects, but, as it were, 'supercharged' with intense even hysterical emotionality; hatred, jealousy, avarice, lust, usually expressed with a marked theatricality.[4]

Melodrama is also an artistic genre, and this negative attitude about excess in emotional responses often carries over to assessments of works in that genre. The criticisms are just as familiar: moral simplification, excessive emotionality, shameless and 'cheap' attempts to manipulate audience emotions (it is no great accomplishment to make any audience very sad by showing the suffering and death of a child), unbelievable plot coincidences and a somewhat primitive style, a lack of refinement in what was presumed to be entirely commercial work, aimed at the 'lowest common denominator'. That is certainly true of very many melodramas, perhaps the overwhelming majority, but to appreciate Sirk, I think we need first to attend to a distinct sub-genre of film melodramas. It is an elusive, unusual category, so it might be best to begin with some examples.

At the end of King Vidor's 1937 classic melodrama, *Stella Dallas*, one of the four or five best instances of the sub-genre, Stella, played by Barbara Stanwyck, having sacrificed or given up her daughter, the core of anything meaningful in her life, to her ex-husband and his

---

[4]For an indispensable summary of the critical and historical literature on melodrama, see Gledhill, 'The Melodramatic Field: An Investigation', in *Home Is Where the Heart Is*, pp. 5–39. She rightly notes early on a basic split in auteurist and mise-en-scène and neostructuralist psychoanalytic and ideology-critique approaches, and so the contrast between the author's intentions expressed in what is said and done and meaning carried more visually and ideologically. Part of the attempt here is to begin to demonstrate why this is a false duality, itself based on the assumption of a Cartesian ideology of the private, self-ownership view of individual mindedness, versus some outside determination. The great value of Sirk's melodramas is to insist on the inseparability of the psychological (including reference to the author's intentions as well as in approaches to characters in the film) and the sociohistorical. But showing this without rendering the former a mere appearance or epiphenomenon of or reducible to the latter is the great dialectical difficulty.

Image 1.1

new family so that she could be raised in a wealthy and cultured environment, watches from outside a large window the wedding of her daughter to another swell in the same society. It is rainy, miserable weather. Stella is treated by a policeman as just another curiosity seeker, and, intensifying what is already a humiliating situation, has to plead with him to remain a few moments longer. (Image 1.1)[5]

After the wedding she then turns and walks toward the camera, drenched and excluded from her daughter's life, but she walks in a way that visually signals pride, triumph and great joy. A happy ending. (Image 1.2)

---

[5]All the images from this film are screengrabs made by me from *Stella Dallas* (1937, The Samuel Goldwyn Company), directed by King Vidor.

Image 1.2

But the scene is also suffused with what seems wholly unnecessary pathos and suffering. While the new step-mother (Helen Morrison, played as saintly by Barbara O'Neill) has taken pains to make sure the curtains of the large window are drawn open, as if it had been planned that Stella must watch from the outside, the gesture only forces us to wonder why Stella, who had raised the daughter Laurel (played somewhat cloyingly by Anne Laurel) could *not* be present at the wedding, must watch in the rain, as if she were watching a film, and in just the sense that critics speak of an ontologically distinct, screened off film world, unenterable. (It is important that as she walks straight toward us, and so she seems to embody us as we leave 'the same' movie theatre; joyous, proud of Stella, smiling. This increases the sense of pathos because we had seen Stella at the beginning of the movie watching people like Helen on screen and telling Stephen she wants to be just like those people. She ends the film still watching and apparently still admiring.) We might assume that her presence would embarrass Laurel, but Stella has already shown, to us and to Laurel and to her ex, Stephen, that she understands perfectly how to dress and act when she is out of her usual environment, and so the general *mise en scène* of the wedding and her exclusion, seems pointlessly cruel. (One imagines the saintly Helen *planning* for Stella to watch from outside, knowing she is watching in the rain. Even if she has convinced herself that 'this is what Stella wants', we are supposed to admire this? 'At least she let her watch'?) And what daughter would *agree* to the exclusion of her supposedly beloved mother? We might assume that Stella would think her presence too painful for Laurel, would make her feel guilty for jumping from one family into another and so disrupt the whole mood of the wedding. But if that is how Laurel might feel, why would it *ease* her guilt to hide her mother away, knowing that that is what she is doing? (If she doesn't know about the window plan, she certainly knows that her mother has not been invited.)[6] Finally, whence the sense of triumph? Stella had married Stephen – we can even say, schemed and manoeuvred to marry Stephen – because she thought that he was her ticket to just such a country club world. It doesn't take her long to realize that such a world is snobbish, self-satisfied, puritanical, hypocritical, vain and intolerant. (The window plan, the exclusion

---

[6]This is a summary. The issues are not clear-cut, and Laurel is hardly a calculating social climber. (She is nowhere near clear enough about herself and her motives for this to be true.) But the exclusion of Stella from the wedding and Laurel's beaming happiness and apparent indifference to this fact are still surprising, to say the least.

from the wedding, seem just to confirm what she sensed about these people.) Stella in effect secedes from that way of living; insists on being Stella, not conforming.[7] But now she seems not only gloriously happy that she had succeeded in getting Laurel into just that world, the one she so justifiably rejected, she has done so while preserving Laurel's delusions and fantasies, the fantasies that have made that world seem so desirable. (There had been an earlier scene where Laurel is so upset that Stella had gotten a tiny bit of cold cream on a picture of the new step-mother-to-be that she almost flies into a rage, almost risks a break with Stella, and Stella does not react, allows Laurel to hold onto her puerile sense of the perfection of the Helen Morrison world.)[8]

So for any attentive viewer the almost universal sense of triumph and joy first conveyed by the scene has a second and then a third moment.[9] The second moment, the suspicion that the ending is far from the happy and affirmed one we first experienced, grows as we realize how out of proportion is the pathos and then pity we are made

---

[7] If in the surface plot Stella seems the 'Madame Bovary of Bolton, Mass', sacrificing daughter and husband to 'go to the ball', then Stephen is very much a 'Charles', dense and eminently 'leave-able'. See J. Segond, 'The Bad and the Beautiful: sur Stella Dallas et le wedding night', *Positif*, Nov. 1974, no. 163, p. 39.

[8] After the flare-up, there is then a loving, reconciliation scene of Laurel helping Stella with her toilet, but it is more suffused with pity than love (Laurel playing mother to her infantile mother) and it increases the strangely unnoticed tension in Laurel's affective economy, inclining to leave her mother to advance herself (despite some hesitation that requires a theatrical push from Stella), but able to avoid any sense that that is what she is doing.

[9] All of this is compatible with Stella's joy being accompanied by a sense of the injustice done her. We don't see evidence of this, but Stella has been canny and insightful throughout the film, and could certainly be happy that Laurel is so happy, and yet stoically aggrieved. My point is that what she is happy about is not necessarily something *we* should be, and that the ending itself is hardly 'happy'.

to feel.[10] What we see, the visual information we first take in, seems to mean one thing, and then, on some reflection, seems to mean another, and that different sense is inconsistent with the first, not simply another 'layer'. (We have to say: *can* seem another meaning. It is characteristic of this sub-genre of melodramas (more on this below) that the majority of audiences and early and even later critics do not experience any second thoughts.) Then, on 'third thought', we have to wonder what the point of this tension is, why we first seem to occupy the point of view of Stella, equally blind to how she has been treated, and then, on second viewing or second thought, attentive to how terribly she has been treated and how little real value there is in the world of horses and vacations and private clubs and spoiled, entitled children that she has succeeded in helping Laurel enter. In general, in the type of melodramas I want to circumscribe, some sort of uneasiness often builds in the viewer as aspects of what we are shown by directorial means seems to conflict with what the characters believe and how they evaluate each other, an unease that is felt most typically when the film ends, in how the narration is (apparently) happily resolved. This will in what follows raise several questions about the point of cinematic irony in some melodramas, but any viewer who

---

[10]For the contrary view, that the film itself does not ironize the submission to patriarchy, but contributes and is meant to contribute to the policing of proper mothering roles in patriarchy, see E. Ann Kaplan, 'The Case of the Missing Mother: Maternal Issues in Vidor's Stella Dallas', in *Feminism and Film*, ed. E. Ann Kaplan (Oxford: Oxford University Press, 2000), pp. 466–78. Stanley Cavell has objected to all such treatments of Stella and has tried to show her active rather than passive role in dealing with and resisting a not nearly good enough world. I don't think his reading can account for the pathos and irony of the ending. See his *Contesting Tears: The Hollywood melodrama of the Unknown Woman* (Chicago: University of Chicago Press, 1997), Chapter Five, 'Stella's taste: Reading Stella Dallas', pp. 197–222).

has experienced the film can at least be sure that that point is not to satirize Stella for her blindness and self-blindness. Something much deeper and more complicated seems at stake.

Take another example. In Max Ophuls's 1949 film *Caught*, Barbara Bel Geddes plays a dreamy former car hop and 'charm school' graduate, Leonora Eames, who, we learn, is captured by fashion magazine and mass culture fantasies of luxury life. (The role of marketing, advertising and the popular press in shaping her fantasies about marriage, romance and women is prominent.) She dreams of marrying well as her escape from the daily grind of working life (as her only escape). And she does stumble haphazardly into an unlikely marriage with a multi-millionaire played by Robert Ryan, Smith Ohlrig, a raving, brutal narcissist who cares nothing for Leonora and only marries her to make a point to his therapist. Leonora is humiliated and lonely in the marriage and finally escapes, taking a job in a doctor's office for poor patients in the Lower East Side. There she meets Dr. Larry Quinada, played by James Mason, a man who appears to be Ohlrig's polar opposite, selfless, dedicated to helping others, indifferent to money and macho displays of strength. Leonora is falling for him, but he seems dissatisfied with her work and she is still married to Ohlrig and is persuaded to return to the latter's mansion for one more try. She sleeps with him, but realizes nothing has changed and goes back to Dr. Quinada. But she learns she is pregnant and returns reluctantly, yet again, to the mansion. A budding romance has already developed with Quinada but so does what should be some audience unease about him. After she has gone missing from the office, there is a scene that stages a discussion between Quinada and his partner about Leonora, conducted across the reception room in a

Image 1.3

way that prominently features the empty chair where Leonora would normally sit. (Ophuls's famous moving camera does not cut simply between the interlocutors but swings by the empty desk and chair to and fro in order to emphasize her absence as the subject of the conversation.) (Image 1.3)

There is thus an implication that the actual Leonora plays as little real role in their speculations and concern as she does to Ohlrig, and this is intensified by the way the conversation goes after Quinada says he actually proposed to Leonora on their first date. His partner[11] suggests, 'Why don't you just forget her?' and Quinada merely says,

---

[11]The partner, Dr. Hoffman, is the OBGYN in the partnership and he knows that Leonora is pregnant, and when he learns that Quinada has only taken Leonora out once, realizes it cannot be his child.

'You think so?'[12] We recall that Quinada can be just as self-satisfied, patronizing and dogmatic in his do-gooder role as Ohlrig was in his own narcissistic lecturing. There are even two scenes that clearly place the two men in parallel. Ohlrig, while he busies himself with billiard balls, lectures Leonora about her job as his wife, explains to her about what she has gotten herself into and tells her how to act, what she's in for. In a remarkable, virtually geometrically staged parallel, the saintly Dr. Quinada, busying himself with medicine bottles, does much the same thing in somewhat the same arrogant tone, hectoring and berating Leonora for thinking she is better than her clientele, even tells her her hair style is inappropriate, that she must do her job better. Leonora wears the same baffled, hurt expression in both scenes.

Finally Quinada goes to the mansion to rescue the pregnant Leonora, even though she at first resists, worried about 'security' for her baby, still committed to the supreme importance of money in life. Ultimately she does leave and suffers a miscarriage. And again, what might be read as a happy ending turns out to be more complicated. In the ambulance, Quinada tells her that her child may die, 'a terrible thing, but you'll be free to start living. Isn't that true?' He tells her that all Ohlrig wanted was to dominate her and kick her around like he does everyone else. 'Now you can be free, free to do all those things that are worthwhile.' Remarkably not once during this speech about how fortunate it is that the baby has died does Leonora look at Quinada. She stares upward, somewhat vacantly (thinking no doubt about the child she had been carrying). Even after he embraces her,

---

[12]*Caught* (1949, MGM), directed by Max Ophuls; screenplay by Arthur Laurents. All the images from this film are screengrabs made by me.

Image 1.4

she does not meet his eyes and simply says the last lines she speaks in the film, a tear escaping from her eye, 'I hear you Larry.' (Image 1.4)

Again, what would almost universally be taken to be a happy ending, Leonora freed from the tyrant Ohlrig, and loved by the saintly Dr. Quinada, is an affective response that should also be disturbed by the memory of these cinematic details; a sense of closure cannot be fully indulged. This disturbance might be quite vague, like the sense one might have after leaving what seemed a happy dinner party that something, as yet unidentifiable, was amiss, that some remark had slid by that more and more comes to seem to have meant something upsetting or that someone left hurriedly in the middle of a conversation in a way that now seems abrupt. Or, we can sense something breaking through a self-deceived view of ourselves, an unease growing, without our at first being able to specify what that is. In such cases, some subjective sense of satisfaction is disturbed. We want to enjoy the liberation of Leonora, and so we leave the theatre or the TV room with some slight alarm going off ('Did James Mason really just say that the death of this child was a good, liberating thing?') but we are overall happy for Leonora and Quinada. The nature of that alarm, what it may mean, cinematically, morally and even politically, will be the subject of these reflections on Sirk.

One last example to help establish that this is something like a sub-genre. In Nicholas Ray's 1955 classic, *Rebel Without a Cause*, James Dean's character, Jim Stark, is tormented by what he experiences as the phoniness, conformism and cowardice of his parents' generation and their middle-class suburban life. So the movie is characterized as one of the best of that 1950s phenomenon, the 'teenage Angst' movie, an exploration that helped establish there was a distinct life-stage between childhood and adulthood, a stage that in the postwar American world was so fraught it was producing dangerous risk-taking behaviour and juvenile delinquency. Much of this 'problem', Jim's most intense suffering, revolves around his relation to his father, played by Jim Backus. The father, Frank Stark, is portrayed as just as weak, 'effeminate', indecisive and terrified of social exclusion as Jim fears he is. In the film's sympathetic expression of Jim's point of view, Ray makes a point about bourgeois society that goes back to at least Rousseau: that this world has no place in it for honour or even integrity, since its supreme values are self-interest and social success (it was precisely a nostalgic yearning for such virtues that terrified Hobbes, who regarded any such commitment as deeply irrational). But the father (siding with Hobbes) argues throughout that Jim doesn't understand the adult world, what is now necessary to survive in it, and that he will only understand when he becomes an adult himself. He tells Jim that all this agony will come to look strange and irrelevant in a few years. The viewer experiences this as Jim does; as hopelessly self-deceived, an excuse for Frank's suppression of his own identity and his cowardice. This is intensified in the way the film presents the relation between Jim's love interest, Natalie Wood's character, Judy, and her father. That parent, played by William Hopper, starts to express what appears to Judy a sudden and incomprehensible withdrawal of all affection, especially physical expression. It is clear and creepy that the father is not only uncomfortable with the fact that his 'little girl' has 'become a woman' (and Judy hardly ever appears in anything but a tight sweater) but that he has developed his own unhealthy interest in her sexuality, is terrified of it, represses it by becoming cold and unresponsive to his daughter; all this as a cost of the hypocritical and repressive characteristics of their social world.

The situation leads to a crisis, the death of the teenage couple's parentally abandoned friend, Plato, played by Sal Mineo, and what appears to be a resolution of the movie's central theme. Over the dead body of the shamefully neglected but also very disturbed and damaged Plato,[13] Jim and his father reconcile. This is already the first 'disturbance' as if – and one has to say 'ironically' – the dead body of Plato (the impossibility of his differences) is some sort of lesson that must learned and worse, accepted, in order to enter adult society. Its potential significance as an indictment of that world is quickly ignored, as Jim, somewhat ceremoniously, enters it by embracing his

---

[13]We are first introduced to Plato as a 'puppy killer', although, remarkably, we seem to forget this in our growing sympathy with Plato's plight.

father. This should call to mind what now starts to appear as the irony in the title of the film. The rebel, we think, must be Jim (James Dean is the star after all), but Jim is not at all without causes; he has plenty: honour, integrity, honesty, rectitude, authenticity and so on. The 'rebel without a cause' is poor Plato. He yearns for loving parents and a humane world, but there is nothing to be done to achieve that; there is no cause to be had. His rebellion is real; a violent rebellion, killing animals, keeping and threatening to use a gun. And as he keeps insisting, rightly, throughout the film: no one can help him. Or as his nanny (actually the housekeeper who generously acts as his nanny) says, 'That poor baby got nobody. Just nobody.' At the end, it is as if Jim finally 'understands' what his father had been saying, that the father is not a coward and a hypocrite but just an adult living in what the adult word now requires.

But this world that Jim now literally embraces has not changed at all. We have no reason to believe any of his father's vow of change and renewal. What looks like reconciliation is rather just the total defeat of Jim's 'rebellion with cause'. Or, rather, this is all a perverse co-option of Jim, not a reconciliation with him. That he and Judy are headed for the same sort of domestic drudgery as his father and mother is signalled in extraordinarily subtly ways by Ray. The coat that Natalie Wood's character, Judy, wears in one of the heart-to-hearts with Jim (Image 1.5) is the same coat we see on Jim's mother at the final planetarium scene (Image 1.6), identifying Natalie with her future role as, and probably nothing other than Mrs Jim Stark. Here the irony is quite bitter; Mrs Stark is one of the least likeable, certainly the least admirable character in the film (unless one counts the mother-in-law).

Image 1.5

Image 1.6

As viewers used to Hollywood endings, we tend to forget, as we listen to Jim's father pledge to become a wholly different person than the one we have seen throughout the film, that there is no reason to believe he can suddenly free himself from the leash held by his wife and mother-in-law.

'You can depend on me. Trust me. Whatever comes, we'll face it together. I swear it. Stand up. I'll stand up with you. I'll try to be as strong as you want me to be.'[14]

---

[14]*Rebel Without a Cause* (1955, Warner Brothers), directed by Nicholas Ray; screenplay by Stewart Stern; adaptation by Irving Shulman, from a story by Nicholas Ray. All the images from this film are screengrabs made by me.

Image 1.7

After Jim introduces Judy to his parents (another sort of ritualized demonstration of adulthood equality), his mother begins to express her usual disapproval and micro-management but the parental couple then smile in some sort of smug self-satisfaction, as if to say to each other, 'We don't need to worry anymore. Jim has become one of us.'

Perhaps these ironic 'disturbances' in the film's ending might explain the otherwise baffling cameo by Ray himself in the last scene of the film, as he is shown approaching the supposed reconciliation not as the artsy director Nick Ray, but as a modern bourgeois businessman, in trench coat and briefcase, a final sign of some unsettling refusal of satisfaction, an ironic sign of the extent of the embourgeoisement that has just occurred that then backshadows the film we have just seen. (Image 1.7)

I don't at all mean to suggest that the films in this sub-genre are pessimistic, sceptical, cynical or satirical. The central feature involves characters who clearly feel they have solved some issue, overcome something, and are enjoying either happiness or the satisfaction of some resolution. Moreover, the social order has been restored to some sort of rightness, or so it would at first appear. The right person seems

to have ended up with the right person, the bad person seems to have
lost out, a disruption has apparently been quieted. And yet, by
cinematic means – staging a mother in the rain, forced to watch her
daughter marry through a window and happy about it; an ambulance
ride with someone voicing a sentiment we have also been induced to
feel but know we shouldn't, talking to someone who never looks at
him; and a ritualized reconciliation that seems both a relief and a great
disappointment – our ability to adopt their point of view is disturbed;
upon more reflection, foreclosed. We seem to know both that their
illusions are the result of some level of blindness about themselves and
their loved ones, but the films manage to make this blindness if not a
sympathetic trait, than an unavoidable one as a defensive measure in
such a social world, and hardly blamable.[15] Their own unknowingness
blunts any easy moral assessment and our sense of the irony of these
endings, an irony that I have suggested characterizes the films in the
sub-genre, then backshadows such films and changes forever how we
watch them at subsequent viewings. This all seems not just a cinematic
technique, or wholly an aesthetic response, but a reaction that leaves
us as viewers where irony often leaves us: in some state of suspended,
deferred, or qualified judgement, one that might even intimate a form
of living appropriate for a society so powerfully able to form its
participants: wary, cautious, attuned to interpretive complexity,
resistant to moralism. But it is yet another mark of these melodramas
though that such reactions are rare, and the films are read in ways that
affirm just what they are ironizing. This is certainly the case with Sirk.

---

[15]Sirk's most extensive and complicated treatment of such blindness is his extended allegory
on the theme, *Magnificent Obsession* (1954).

The German émigré director Douglas Sirk, born Hans Detlef Sierk, led an interesting and complicated life, but for our purposes, there are three salient facts. The first is that he must have been one of the most highly educated of all the émigré directors working in Hollywood. He studied at Jena and Hamburg, mostly philosophy, art history and painting, was a star student of Erwin Panofsky, wrote his own translations of Shakespeare's sonnets, worked as a set designer and dramaturge and soon after university became one of the most prominent theatre directors in Germany, mostly left-wing and avant-garde theatre in Bremen, Chemnitz, Hamburg and Leipzig, and especially the plays of Bertolt Brecht. Second, after he emigrated from Germany in 1937 (his second wife was Jewish, although that story is another long one), he found work for a while in Europe, and for a long time found very little in Hollywood. He even tried his hand at chicken farming and when that failed, alfalfa farming. That failed too. (Sirk's German experience in the 1930s remained a touchstone for him. He has said that he wanted to focus on the American middle class, because it was there, in that class, that Hitler took root. And Sirk saw disturbing similarities.) But in 1952 he teamed up with the producer Ross Hunter at Universal Studios, and until he repatriated to Europe in 1959 (and stopped making films) he made a string of financially successful melodramas, the most famous of which were *Magnificent Obsession*, *All That Heaven Allows*, *All I Desire*, *There's Always Tomorrow*, *Written on the Wind*, *Tarnished Angels* and *Imitation of Life*. Eventually, the total number of films he made was thirty-nine.

The third fact concerns the reception history of Sirk and melodrama in general. Until the 1970s, Sirk's films, as well as those by Ophuls and other melodramatists, were considered stylish but thoroughly commercial films for a mass public; their directors were assumed to be making movies for a gullible, naïve, simplistic audience. These films were contemptuously dismissed as mere 'women's pictures' or 'weepies', soap operas or tear-jerkers.

But two things happened in the 1970s. The first was the rise of feminist criticism, which of course asked pointedly why a characterization of a film as a 'woman's picture' should be a disparagement. A realization grew that films made about and for women amounted to that rarest of phenomena in mass culture: the articulation of a woman's point of view, especially women suffering largely at the hands of ignorant, narcissistic men. The disparagement of films so intently about women as overwrought emotionally and simplistic, began to seem like the verdict of the patriarchy, unfair and exclusionary. Much of the early wave of such criticism was more sociological than aesthetic criticism, but it focused a great deal of intense, careful attention on these films, including Sirk's. Secondly, in 1971, the critic Jon Halliday published a series of illuminating interviews with Sirk in which he patiently explained the ironic and subversive nature of his melodramas, and his paramount interest in style and formal matters. French critics in the *Cahiers du cinéma* crowd, especially François Truffaut, had already in the 1950s discovered Sirk as a major auteur, but he was still dismissed in America until these interviews. (One sure sign, finally taken some note of, that Sirk's melodramas at Universal Studios might not be all they initially seem is the immediate ambiguity of the titles of many of the most ambitious ones. For example, the 1955 film, *All That Heaven Allows* could suggest, 'Look at all that heaven allows in its generosity.' And it could mean, 'Be careful. This paltry consolation or happiness, and this alone, is all that heaven allows.' In interviews Sirk made clear he meant the latter, that for him, 'heaven is stingy', and he was amused that the studio gave it the former interpretation. They thought it a brilliant, uplifting title.[16] Many other films throughout his American career have the same double character: *Imitation of Life*, *Tarnished Angels*, *All I Desire* and *There's Always Tomorrow*.) Critics remembered the European Sirk and could begin to see the strongly Brechtian aesthetic of the films.[17] That is, the films were clearly anti-realist and anti-naturalistic. A realist film, like those, say, by John Ford or Orson Welles, is designed to be recognizable to the audience as continuous with their own experience; the movie screen is supposed to be transparent, as if we are, unobserved, looking directly at what is happening. Sirk's melodramas are nothing like this. The set design consists of slick, glossy colours and the colour scheme is extreme, like nothing one would ordinarily see, and we notice all this artifice as much as what we see happening. In effect, we could say we see the director's intentions, how his style tells us why he is telling the story this way, as much as the story itself.[18] ('Hollywood baroque' was one term coined to describe Sirk's style.) Anti-naturalism means that characters' psychological affect is exaggerated; the dramatic action often goes beyond what is realistically acceptable; plot events are

---

[16]Cf. 'Or take *All That Heaven Allows* . . . The studio loved the title; they thought it meant you could have everything you wanted. I meant it exactly the other way round. As far as I am concerned, heaven is stingy.' J. Halliday, *Sirk on Sirk: Conversations with Jon Halliday* (London: Faber and Faber, 1971), p. 140. He goes on to make similar points about other titles.

[17]It is generally accepted now, especially in film studies, that Sirk managed to create an artifice that 'comments on the world, as it comments on the means of representation', Barbara Klinger, *Melodrama and Meaning: History, Culture, and the Films of Douglas Sirk* (Bloomington, Ind., 1994), p. 9. Klinger's book is indispensable on the various receptions of Sirk and on the significance of that variation.

[18]On anti-realism in melodramas in general, see C. Gledhill, 'The Melodramatic Field: An Investigation', p. 5.

implausible. Characters are bizarrely self-destructive. The music is intense and not subtle. Some films have a kind of mood of hysteria running through them.

Although most melodramas made in the Hollywood system do not merit serious attention as works of art, however interesting they may be sociologically or culturally, several directors, many of them European, like Douglas Sirk, Max Ophuls, Vincente Minnelli, Michael Curtiz, managed to work in the melodrama genre and make what I at least consider world-class works of cinematic art. Not all of the superb ones fit into this ironic category, the 'second-thought melodramas'. In some the intensity of the emotional tonality achieved by cinematic and musical means matches the intensity of the suffering the characters experience. George Steven's 1951 *A Place in the Sun* is a fine example, as is Irving Rapper's *Now, Voyager* (1942). There are 'extreme' melodramas too, like Lars von Trier's *Breaking the Waves* where the events are so horrific that there is no 'exaggerated' or 'excessive' response possible. In very good and great melodramas like *A Place in the Sun*, the ending is straightforwardly sad or restorative, reconciling, never undercut. In the following I will focus on three films by Sirk that do seem to me to exemplify the sub-genre I have been describing.

As in past books on film, the point will also be to demonstrate that appreciating how Sirk understood the resources of melodrama can shed light on how films can have a bearing on, help illuminate, important philosophical issues. Now, there is an active dispute among philosophers interested in film about whether film, or some films, should be considered a form of philosophy itself, or is better understood as an aid to philosophy, suggesting something like thought-experiments, or illustrations and examples of philosophical problems, or as inspiring philosophical analysis. This debate can become quite confusing very quickly because there is very little consensus even among professional philosophers about what philosophy itself is. The putative charge that films can't be modes of philosophy because they don't result in philosophical knowledge and don't even reach conclusions is quite misleading since it is absurd to assume that philosophy itself issues in philosophical knowledge (there is very little consensus in philosophy about anything, as there would be if 'knowledge' had been reached), and conclusions reached on the basis of arguments in philosophy descend from assumed premises already as controversial as the conclusions. Others claim that films alone cannot be philosophical because any cinematic version of philosophical self-consciousness depends on the interpretation of the films, and that must be where philosophical work goes on. But if interpretation is successful, it must be a way of bringing to greater self-consciousness what is in the film, how the film can direct us to think about some issue one way rather than another. Moreover, and most simply put, on the Socratic conception of philosophy, long one of the most influential in the history of thought, we need to be brought to understand matters that we believe (and since belief tracks truth, that we take to be true) that are so close to us that we don't know we believe them, and don't realize our stake in their truth, and there are matters that we take ourselves to believe that we actually don't, or believe because we need to or want to, or don't realize have necessary implications that we would disavow. There is no reason to deny that films can contribute to these ends, philosophical ends, and so no reason to deny them the status of philosophy, even if one wants, for the sake of some purity, to insist that they amount to philosophy by other means. For what we need illuminated are issues that are not available to us as direct objects of traditional philosophical analysis. These are questions that only emerge within a human life world, some horizon of significance, or form of life so deeply presupposed that it only becomes available to us if there is some way of coming to understand 'what it is like' for interacting subjects to be called on to make judgements about others, trust others, rely on some piece of putative self-knowledge, come to feel 'alienated' from a social world, feel disrespected, assess what a lack of standing in a world means to them, whether they are in love or not, whether a profession of confidence or friendship is reliable and so forth. We could call this all a phenomenology of the life world made available by great films as long as we don't invoke that term to marginalize it; that is realize that the content of a number of crucial concepts of interest to philosophy have the content they have only as so experienced, and at a time, and we need some access to such a life world to begin to understand the borders and relations among such concepts, or in some cases whether the concepts have any real content at all. This seems to me all we need to claim justifiably that some films can be considered forms of philosophy.

Given the widespread view of all melodrama as demotic, even vulgar forms of art, invoking such a notion for that genre might sound implausible, but it should not be surprising. Melodramas often concern two of the most powerful aspirations and ideals in modern bourgeois life: the desire to love and to be loved, and the desire for a measure of standing, or status, respect; an acknowledgement as a worthwhile contributor to, as valued in, one's social world. In modern consumer societies, this is often taken to be a matter of financial security, and so a demonstration of one's competitive success, but the limitations of that narrow a sense of status are legendary. In the films explored below, Sirk focuses quite critically on different sources of such standing available in Eisenhower's America. In *All That Heaven Allows*, it is social class, taken so seriously that it leads to an anxious and destructive policing of the boundaries of class, especially with respect to romantic 'appropriateness'. In *Written on the Wind*, Sirk explores the importance of moral rectitude as a source of self-satisfaction, one that can compensate for the absence of great wealth or for the banal character of daily life, but which also makes self-deceit and hypocrisy inevitable. In *Imitation of Life*, he explores the attractions of fame and celebrity status, or more simply, being regarded as one wants to be regarded, as well as a far uglier source of standing in this bourgeois world, race.

In these explorations, it is surely philosophically important to be able to ask: what is it people mean when they place such a high value on love? What is it to want to love and be loved? How is that that people come to find their standing in the world satisfactory or unsatisfactory? And especially, if there is some evidence that these desiderata cannot be well satisfied in a historical form of life, why might that be? As just noted, a form of life and its many dimensions cannot be an object *in* such a life and not available for philosophy as a set of beliefs or concepts to be analysed. 'What it is like' to be the subjects of these problems is not available as a set of data either. And a cinematic expression of what it is so like or what it is to want such things is not a mere reservoir of evidence for philosophy. In the way the story is narrated, the characters presented, the scenes edited, the framing organized, the sound and music created, a point of view is taken, one that can only be credible if the narration itself is credible, if we can recognize some undistorted revelatory view of ourselves in what we see. Again, it has been said from Socrates to Wittgenstein that philosophy does not produce new results, new knowledge, but helps us see what we already knew and did not know we did. If that is a task of philosophy, why should film not be a major means for doing so?

Sirk has a distinctive and illuminating sense of how and why these two aspirations can, indeed almost inevitably must, conflict in the kind of world we have made and can thus reveal something important about the politics of emotional life. That is, emotional states like resentment, revulsion, shame and jealousy have specific contents, objects. Those contents are the result of some interpretive work. Emotions like these are reactive; reactions depend on what we think we perceive, and what we think we perceive is often the result of interpretations of what was said or done by another. These interpretations are functions of commonly held social conventions, norms, and can be quite sensitive to the structure of power and influence in a society. A certain form of social life, industrial and consumer capitalism, for example, because of the social bases of self- and other-respect that it demands, also requires and produces a certain economy in a soul's affective states, and it is obviously a matter of philosophical interest how that works. This theme is as old as Plato's *Republic*. Socrates argues there that certain regimes require (create and sustain) certain types of soul; tyrannical regimes one sort, democratic regimes another sort, aristocratic regimes another. We might not invoke the notion of soul nowadays, and prefer to speak of certain habits of mind, characteristic dispositions, predictable and manipulable affective responses and so forth, but Sirk's films and many other melodramas help raise an elusive philosophical question: what sorts of souls do modern middle-class, mass culture, consumerist, liberal democratic capitalist societies require, create and sustain?

There is an 'objective' as well as a 'subjective' dimension to Sirk's treatment. The social worlds depicted in some of Sirk's melodramas are often all pretence, theatre, wholly false, conformist role-playing phoniness.[19] This means of course that they are often simply hypocritical, but the important players often seem to believe the theatre and see none of their own falseness. The garishness of Sirk's presentation of such worlds always appears to suggest that this world, a clearly artificial world – no natural colours look like the ones we see – a world presented as if a bright ad in a slick magazine, or a television show in early colour, is some sort of projection of *the characters' own sense of themselves*, how *they* see themselves, posed with an intensity that intimates a lingering anxiety and so defensiveness about authenticity, genuine individuality or self-realization and, in the majority of cases, about the possibility of love in such a world. We shall return to this issue below; this projective feature could be called the cinematic equivalent of what is 'free indirect discourse' in literature, a third-person visual narration that describes or, here depicts, as if from a first-person consciousness. This occurs when say, an omniscient narrator reports something like, 'He looked into her tender, lovely lying eyes', momentarily adopting in the third person the first-person experience of the character. Here we have a projection

---

[19]There is a good discussion of 'pretending' as 'the main attribute of American middle-class life' in R. Rushton, 'Douglas Sirk's Theatres of Imitation', in *Screening the Past*, Issue 21 (2007), p. 1.

of a staged, theatrical phoniness, unaware of itself as such. That is a remarkable technical achievement.[20]

What also distinguishes melodramas by Sirk is a feature one certainly finds in other melodramas (for example, some by Minnelli and Ophuls, and a few by the Dardenne brothers like *The Silence of Lorna* and *The Unknown Girl*): the establishment of a connection between that element prominent in all melodrama, the suffering of women, with a social critique of that common world; a critique accomplished simply by its noticeably distanced depiction, as a context within which that suffering is both more intelligible, more painful and almost inevitable.[21] His focus on what are clearly regarded as the pathologies of Eisenhower's 1950s America is essential to understand the enormous attractiveness of the promise of love, both romantic and familial, and for Sirk its inevitable failure, a failure at the intimate level shown as to be expected in such a social world, and often masked in self-deceit.

The main feature of the Sirkian sub-genre identified above raises a number of questions of its own. *How* a cinematic style can be ironic, how what we are shown can suggest how much is not shown, perhaps the contrary of what is shown, is a fascinating topic in itself, and there are many different examples of how it works[22]: Nicholas Ray's *Johnny Guitar*, Josef von Sternberg's *The Scarlet Empress*, and Stanley Kubrick's *Barry*

---

[20]Of course, this is not the only effect of such style. Elsaesser is surely right that the meaning of what we see in family film melodramas and especially in Sirk is to a great degree a matter of décor, lighting, music, camera movement, composition of frame, colour and gesture. See T. Elsaesser, 'Tales of Sound and Fury', p. 52. But seeing such matters as also an analogue of free indirect discourse helps destabilize the dualism mentioned above in n. 4.

[21]See again, Elsaesser, ibid., on melodramas recording 'the struggle of a morally and emotionally emancipated bourgeois consciousness against the remnants of feudalism' (with the bourgeois rich playing the Victorian role of aristocrats), p. 45

[22]For a fine discussion, see James MacDowell, 'Interpretation, Irony, and "Surface Meanings" in Film', *Film-Philosophy* 22, no. 2 (2018): 261–80 and his *Irony in Film* (London, 2016).

Lyndon, just to name three examples. And whether Sirk, in those surprisingly forthcoming interview remarks about his own films, was simply riding the wave of interpretation begun by Truffaut and the *Cahiers* group, or expressing his own, independent views, he did claim that the effect he wanted was a tight connection between genre, structure and style, on the one hand, and 'such themes as failure, impotence, and the impossibility of happiness' on the other,[23] all of which latter are not easily visible on the surface. (He is though alerting us to the fact that the meaning of these pessimistic themes are carried by *mise en scène*, lighting, costumes, colour, camera movement and framing, and not by dialogue or plot.) And to Sirk's despairing list we can add 'the precariousness of love in the American social world he depicts', my topic in the following. In the next chapter, our question will concern first the ways in which the policing of sexual conventions intersects with the policing of class boundaries, and all of that will be shown to make the realization of anything like love, at least any love that is not strictly norm-bound, at best terribly fraught, at worst, impossible. Second, the hope is to understand better the attractiveness in this kind of social world of the contrasting ideal of authenticity, or related phenomena like genuineness, nonconformism, and self-reliance in American life, and to explore briefly the naïveté of a common understanding of that ideal, and the consequences of that naïveté.[24] Finally, these two topics taken together

---

[23]This is Barbara Klinger's summary of Halliday's Introduction to *Sirk on Sirk* in her *Melodrama and Meaning*, p. 9. I tend to give Sirk credit for his independence in the remarks, given his own involvement with avant-garde and left-wing theatre in Germany, but nothing I say in the following depends on evidence from the interviews.

[24]This raises the issue of a properly political psychology. For a discussion of the nature of this problematic, see the Introduction to my *Hollywood Westerns and American Myth: The Importance of Howard Hawks and John Ford for Political Philosophy* (New Haven: Yale University Press, 2010), pp. 1–25.

will raise a different dimension of irony in Sirk's (or the film's) point of view with regard to the events and characters depicted. For just as melodrama is more than a classificatory genre, rather a narrative form that frames and interrogates such issues as the meaning of suffering, conflict, the absence of satisfying love, and the lack of resolution of basic conflict (it is the modern analogue of, or even displacement of, tragedy in this respect), so irony, as suggested above, is more than a literary or cinematic device. It is a kind of ethical stance as well, a way of bearing such contingency and frustration; a 'right' way of coming to terms with our subjection to contingency and failure. This immediately sounds like a recommendation for distance, noninvolvement, playful, mere spectatorship.[25] But, as we shall see, that would be superficial and unresponsive to the unique play of irony in the film. Indeed, the cinematic expression of this sort of irony – simply put, our inability to accept, rest content, with what the film actually seems to be showing us – figures a kind of general, orienting attitude; general because its repetition in this sub-genre suggests the broad difficulty of living in a social world where a kind of blindness, self-deceit and comfort in superficiality are not individual pathologies but inevitable products of that world, necessary for its survival, exposed critically simply by its honest depiction.

So it would be wrong to suggest that the films are best characterized simply as a negatively ironic depiction of such impossibility, failure or frustration. Again, the irony is not mocking or sarcastic. Many of the characters are well-meaning and earnest, even if also fit subjects for an ironic treatment, for our never being able to take at face value what

---

[25]For further discussion, see 'Prologue: Film and Philosophy' in my *The Philosophical Hitchcock: Vertigo and the Anxieties of Unknowingness* (Chicago: The University of Chicago Press, 2017), pp.1–12.

they say and do. That is, aside from the purely visual dimensions of irony, that dimension of artificial colour, lighting and close-up overheated expressions of emotion, all understood as an expression of and so a comment on the febrile state of the characters' emotional lives, there is a more subtle dimension of such estranging irony. We see characters who sincerely avow what they believe, but who have no substantive idea about what in fact they are actually avowing, what the implications would be (the invocation of clichés – e.g. 'to thine own self be true' – is a sure sign of this dim apprehension), or characters whose expressed self-understanding is clearly a manifestation of a self-ignorance; again, even if also sincere and well-meaning.[26] Often we simply *see* that they don't understand what they say or feel, that they even confuse themselves. And such irony also functions as a kind of cinematic, reflective interrogation of just why, in that specific world of 1950s America, romantic love and even familial love should be so fraught. It is this focus that, as we shall see, allows the film to be both a genuine melodrama and a reflective interrogation of the form itself as the form most appropriate to illuminating a certain sort of socio-political world, the modern,

[26]Cf. the remarks in J,-L. Comolli and P. Narboli in 'Cinema/Ideology/Criticism', reprinted from *Cahiers du Cinéma* in *Screen*, 12 (1) (1971): about an ideology critique internal to a film, otherwise quite conventional: 'An internal criticism is taking place which cracks the film apart at the seams. If one reads the film obliquely, looking for symptoms; if one looks beyond its apparent formal coherence, one can see that it is riddled with cracks; it is splitting under an internal tension which is simply not there in an ideologically innocuous film ... This is the case with many Hollywood films, for example, which while being completely integrated in the system and the ideology end up by partially dismantling the system from within.' p. 33. See also P. Willemen on a 'distance between the film and its narrative pretext', in, 'Distanciation and Douglas Sirk', in *Screen*, 12 (2) (1971).

bourgeois American world.[27] In that sense, even the designation melodrama is misleading, since the film is both an invocation of and an ironizing of melodrama as a sense-making form of human experience. They might all be called meta-melodramas, another effect of the irony in the sub-genre we have been exploring.[28]

---

[27]There is a helpful account of the historical conditions and the internal social contradictions so appropriate for melodramatic film, by D.N. Rodowick, 'Madness, Authority and ideology: The Domestic Melodrama of the 1950s', in *Home is Where the Heart Is: Studies in Melodrama and the Woman's Film*, pp. 268–80.

[28]There is an important sense, explored by Cavell, that all Hollywood genres have a meta-generic dimension, that genres are not structures with features to which later instances 'add on' features; that genres are occasions for reimagining the genre. See Cavell's *The Pursuits of Happiness. The Hollywood Comedy of Remarriage* (Cambridge: Harvard University Press, 1981), pp. 28–30.

2

Love and Class in
All That Heaven Allows

But what I fear, what anyone today could grasp if he wanted to, is
that we modern men are on the same path, and each time someone
begins to discover the extent to which he is playing a role, and the
extent to which he can be an actor, he becomes an actor.
NIETZSCHE, *The Gay Science* §356[1]

As opposed to other fast-paced films like *Written on the Wind* and
Imitation of Life, not much actually happens in *All That Heaven*
Allows. It seems reasonable to divide the film into four 'acts', as it were.
In the first act, we are introduced to the small New England town
where the action occurs, Stoningham, clearly a very well-off bedroom
community likely near New York, and already somewhat of a parody
of 'small town' or 'village' America. That view of the 'real' country that
still has such a powerful hold today.[2] The film begins with an aerial

---

[1]Friedrich Nietzsche, *Die fröhliche Wissenschaft*, in *Sämtliche Werke*. Studien Ausgabe. Bd. 3.
Ed. G. Colli and M. Montinari (Berlin: de Gruyter,1988). My translation.
[2]The town's self-image seems to be as a haven from the city, and for many, like Ron and his
friends, as a site of authenticity. See James Harvey, *Movie Love in the Fifties* (Cambridge: Da
Capo Press, 2001), p. 374. The two Thoreauvians in the film, Ron and Mick, seem to assume
that no urban job can be an authentic one, and that unless one lives in a village, and has
some job connected with the commodification of nature, one is doomed to falseness.

shot, a supervisory or monitoring position from a church tower, although religion is never mentioned in the film. There is no priest or minister (that role has been taken over by the doctor), and it is not until very late in the film that we see a cross on the top of the tower, as if to signal its insignificance. We meet right away the main players, Cary Scott (Jane Wyman), a widow with two grown children off at college. (The son comes home on the weekends from Princeton; her daughter goes to Columbia.) Wyman was thirty-eight when the film appeared, but she is styled to look a few years older, and her circle of friends looks older still. That the romance begins in autumn, with leaves falling off trees, is no doubt her image of her 'last chance' at erotic, not companionate love, a first example of the way the film projects a character's self-understanding and in this case her own somewhat ironic sense of herself. And there is that 'smouldering fire' visible as we approach her house. (Image 2.1)[3]

The children are named Kay (Gloria Talbot) and the truly odious Ned (William Reynolds). There is Cary's love interest, Ron Kirby (Rock Hudson), a local gardener and beginning tree farmer, and we meet assorted town folk: Cary's best friend Sara Warren (Agnes Moorehead), the town gossip with the apposite name of Mona Plash (Jacqueline Dewitt), and a pleasant enough bore named Harvey (Conrad Nagel), who, everyone seems to assume, will one day or another end up marrying Cary. In this act, Cary and Ron meet and there is some sport of spark between them, despite the fact (or perhaps because of it) that Cary is older than Ron and a widow with grown

---

[3] *All That Heaven Allows* (1955, Universal), directed by Douglas Sirk; screenplay by Peg Fenick, from a story by Edna L. and Harry Lee. All screengrabs from this film were made by me.

Image 2.1

children. The source of the obvious wealth in the community is not unacknowledged, not even spoken of by anyone, but everyone is clearly well off.

In the second act, Cary and Ron grow very quickly much closer and a real romance begins. Cary discovers that Ron thinks of himself as a nonconformist, a free spirit whose friend Mick reads Thoreau. ('Mick's bible' and we assume, Ron's as well.)[4] Cary has become intrigued by Ron and what appears to be his indifference to the social stratification of the town and his love of nature. Ron may very well be the first person outside her social class that Cary has ever known personally and she is eager to know more about him. He seems to be bringing out some implicit dissatisfaction in herself about her life. So she questions Mick's wife, Alida (Virginia Grey) about Ron and his friend Mick. Alida explains that Mick had become bored and

---

[4]We are told that Ron doesn't have to read the book; he already lives it. But as we shall see, that is not quite right. He not only lives it, he preaches it, and rather self-righteously too.

frustrated with his advertising job in the city and threw it all over for the small nursery he runs; that is, for a simpler life, inspired she says, by Thoreau's *Walden*. Cary, obviously unfamiliar with the book or its ideas, picks it up and begins to read. It is hard to miss the irony of Cary, in a somewhat bewildered tone, reading the famous 'quiet desperation passage'. Two well-off upper middle-class women, highly styled and made up, read approvingly (and in Cary's case, in a somewhat bewildered tone) about silent despair and independence of mind.[5] (Image 2.2)

We learn that Ron has somewhat bohemian friends (at least by the rigidly middle-class attitudes of the town, and, more importantly, in their own eyes) and will soon stop gardening and working for the town folk and open his own tree farm. He lives in his greenhouse and has a confident but sometimes smug and self-satisfied air about him (the first signs of trouble with this character, as we shall see). Cary seems quite taken by Ron, although it is not clear how much of that has to do with his independent ideas or the sexual charge she clearly feels (for her, always somewhat surprisingly) when she is first around him. She does not actually embrace his Thoreauvian philosophy and even at one point assumes he will live in her old house, that her life will go on as before with Ron added on. However, we had already heard some complaints from her about the issue of convention and its

---

[5]Harvey, *Movie Love in the Fifties*, p. 374. The theme of such independence is introduced in an already qualified way. Alida says that Mick was very unhappy working in the city and their marriage almost split up because of his unhappiness. They moved here to live their Thoreauvian life and all is now well. She never says whether *she* was unhappy in New York, whether she wanted this sort of life, is happier here, etc. While she seems happy enough, her life is a kind of 'imitation of life', of Mick's life. The shadow of the war, mentioned a few times (Mick and Ron were wartime buddies), hangs over the narrative too; as if that experience intensifies the need for finding something authentic and genuine in life.

Image 2.2

restrictions. When discussing with her daughter the ancient Egyptian custom of burying the wife alive with the dead husband in his tomb, her daughter says that we don't do that anymore, and Cary says sardonically, 'At least not in Egypt.'[6] This act is the most complicated and involves contrasting evening parties, at the country club and among Ron's happy-go-lucky friends. Of major importance is an old mill near Ron's greenhouse that Cary encourages him to renovate. (Images 2.3 and 2.4)

(The relevance of an ageing run-down building, to be renovated by Ron's loving attention, to their romance is not subtle. There is also a Wedgewood teapot, broken, to be lovingly repaired by Ron, that also fills such a romantic function.) Ron eventually proposes, and after several minutes of terrified deliberation, Cary accepts. The couple

---

[6]Later in the film, this fate is suggested by a scene after the breakup which shows Cary behind a window, as if behind bars, as if trapped by them, staring out and weeping, and in that only image where she looks directly at her image, she seems trapped *inside* the television set purchased for her at Christmas by her children, as if, bizarrely, a husband substitute.

Image 2.3

Image 2.4

announce their engagement to the children and to Sara and all hell
breaks loose.

The third act documents this chaos. The children are appalled, and
immediately reject the choice of Ron as unworthy of their father's
memory, and as an invitation to cruel gossip. ('People will say this all
started before father died.') Her best friend is gentler but still tells
Cary she is making a very bad mistake. The full supervisorial and

Image 2.5

disciplining techniques in the town for conforming behaviour to the norm are called into play. The chief weapons are gossip and catty remarks and her manipulative, self-centred and self-deceived children. On the son's part, it rises to a promise to break with his mother forever and never return. Note the extraordinary, cold blue palette of that scene, (Image 2.5) and the contrast with the scene with her daughter, which is much more emotional and pained, as she pleads with her mother, in a kind of emotional blackmail, not to marry.[7] (Image 2.6)

The cruelty and insensitivity of the children are the most dramatic and shocking aspects of this part of the movie. (Cary somehow does not ever manage to see clearly the selfishness and thoughtlessness of the children.) Feeble efforts to dress Ron up like a country club type (again Cary is clueless about what she is asking Ron to do, how

[7]See the discussion in J. Mercer and M. Shingler, *Melodrama: Genre, Style, Sensibility* (London: Wallflower, 2004), p. 56 and p. 63.

Image 2.6

impossible the theatrical role is that she has assigned him),[8] and to introduce him to that world are catastrophic failures, but not because Ron is standoffish or explicitly judgemental, but because of the thoughtlessness and sarcasm of the townsfolk. Cary finally cannot stand the pressure, caves in, and wants to wait a while. Ron refuses and they break up.

In the fourth act we see that they are both miserable apart, but each seems too proud to compromise. The break in the stalemate comes, tellingly, from Cary's doctor, a new sort of authority in this world, whom she had gone to see about her general lethargy and headaches. His medical advice is simple, 'Marry him, Cary.' What's wrong with the repression the town demands is not, he assumes, that it is unjust,

---

[8] See Fred Camper, 'The Films of Douglas Sirk', in *Screen*, 12 (2) (1971): 'In a sense, then, all characters in Sirk are totally blind, surrounded as they are, not by real things but by falseness. There is no question of seeing "reality" on any level or attaining any genuine understanding since such concepts are completely excluded by the formal qualities of Sirk's images.' p. 48.

conformist, intolerant or unfair, but simply that it is making Cary sick.[9] This is decisive for Cary, although her vision of the kind of life her children want her to lead, married to the sexless Howard and watching endless hours of television, has clearly already shaken her up as well.

She rushes to Ron's renovated mill, but he is out hunting and she loses her nerve anyway and does not knock. (This is quite an important fact that most viewers, eager for a stereotypical happy ending, can easily miss; can want to miss. It signals in effect that there can be no reconciliation until, as we shall see, Ron is in some sense broken, weakened, brought to ground.) Ron is returning home, sees her, and frantically tries to signal her (no hesitation on his part), falling off a high ledge in the process and knocking himself unconscious, seriously injuring himself. In the last scene, as he recovers, they seem reunited, but we recall that she was still afraid to reconcile, has had this reconciliation in effect forced on her by events, and we see an ending that is quite complexly ambiguous. We will look closely at the scene later.

I have mentioned that the portrayal of the 'world of the town Stoningham' is presented in a way that is unmistakably ironic, and in that way, quite critical. The veneer of civility and friendliness is thin. This already suggests that the American pathology that Sirk is examining is dual. It is *both* an anxiety-fuelled, defensive and often ruthless and sadistic obsession with sexual repression and conformism, *as well as* a compensatory Thoreauvian fantasy of self-sufficiency and

---

[9]The doctor asks: 'Do you expect me to give a prescription for life?' This is obviously a rhetorical question, to which the answer is supposed to be No. But he then proceeds to do exactly that: give her a life prescription. The equivalent existential problem for Ron after the breakup is that he 'can't shoot straight', and so is 'good for nothing'. This suggests he can't really be a man occupying the position of a patriarchal relation to Cary. As he probably sees it, he was dumped by her, and so it would be unmanly to make the first move.

independence, and the two are clearly linked. That is, Sirk seems to be presenting the love affair as a supposed brave rejection of such conformism, and as embodying the Thoreauvian philosophy behind the rejection, but there is, in the details of the affair, a much more subtle, but equally deep irony, and I want now to develop that basic point, a point I take to concern not just Ron and his friends, but an American self-understanding in general, captured at its best and worst in a facile understanding of Thoreau. This is so, although establishing it with any confidence would require a look at several other Sirk films.[10] The full claim would be that Sirk treats America's deepest understanding of itself, its self-narration, as a kind of melodrama. That is, if there is such a thing as an American imaginary (and there is very little else that could account for a social bond in a nation state with very little in the way of nation), that imaginary has its own complex psychological roots and dynamics, and essentially involves some collectively understood self-narration; a whence and whither structure that informs everything from acceptable social behaviour (including marriage norms) and the norms of civility to explicit political discourse. Perhaps it would be safer to say that at least one significant version of such a collective self-understanding is melodramatic, and that version is what interests Sirk. Cinematically, it can also be heroic and so epic, as in Westerns; romantic,

---

[10]There is almost always some indication in Sirk's films of some specific barrier, impediment, to a more humane life of social solidarity and sensitivity. Underneath what the ironic treatment reveals, there is something to be recovered, remembered. In this film the barrier is some sort of anxiety about sexual and class boundaries, treated as linked. In *Imitation of Life*, it is the fantasy of fame or the dominance of celebrity culture (also treated with great pathos in *All I Desire*). In *Written on the Wind*, it is a fantasy about masculinity and status. In *Tarnished Angels*, an airplane race figures the effects of obsessive competitiveness. In *There's Always Tomorrow*, it is the deadening habits of domesticity itself.

as in many musicals; and tragic as in the depiction of the fate of postwar urban life in film noirs.[11] This is a large topic, but a national self-conception as virtuous and authentic (liberated from a corrupt and dissembling Europe) under attack and damaged and misunderstood just because of those virtues, resulting in the typical excess of the melodramatic imagination: paranoia, either a fantasy of grandiosity and triumph, or a paranoia of persecution by hidden conspiratorial forces, an overheated, excessively emotional political rhetoric, wishful and fantasy thinking, an exaggerated sanctification of the family and so a mistrust of the public or urban sphere, are not unfamiliar to any American, especially now.[12]

In the first act, as I've called it, the important scenes are the first meeting, her coded reaction to it, and her tentative steps toward a romance. When her friend cancels lunch, Cary, on an apparent impulse, invites her gardener, Ron, to that prepared lunch. He accepts a couple of dinner rolls, and she asks him polite questions about tree farming (playing in effect 'the clueless female'). The soundtrack and

---

[11]For a fuller account of the latter, see my *Fatalism in American Film Noir: Some Cinematic Philosophy* (Charlottesville: University of Virginia Press, 2012). The ultimate philosophical goal of such an approach is to show the poverty of any social or political philosophy – that is any evaluation of the organized use of power by one group against others, with a claim to legitimacy – that does not take into account the individual and collective psychological dimensions of allegiance and especially the malformations or even pathologies typically produced in the societal mechanisms used to insure the internalization of such allegiance; here by the American family in its reproduction of the repressive values assumed to be necessary for order and predictability in Eisenhower's America in the 1950s.

[12]These are characteristics of melodrama (which he calls a 'version of experience' and is linked with tragedy as a 'literature of disaster') in R. Heilman's *Tragedy and Melodrama*, Seattle and London: University of Washington Press, 1968), although not with respect to films, and never with respect to national character. (His basic idea is a valuable one; that, like tragedy, melodrama can be considered more than a genre characterization, but 'an aspect of life', p.3.

his story about the Chinese tree tell us there is more going on than a tree lecture, and we see her disappointment flash quickly across her face when Ron has to leave. Throughout, as here, Ron is associated with nature, and so with the naturalness of Cary's aroused desire, something she will never quite be able to admit to herself in that form.

We also see in the opening scenes an example of a frequent technique in the film, one much commented on in analyses of Sirk: the use of mirrors to suggest the reflective status of the film itself. We see not only the movie world, we see (or we should see) that it is represented in a way, or we see ourselves seeing in such a distinct way (the cinematic irony has the same effect). The technique also opens the question of whether and if so how the characters see not just their world but how they are taking, imagining that world to be. So we see the chance for, and the lack of, reflection on the part of someone. Cary sits in front of mirrors a few times, but in the scene depicted here and in all the others in front of mirrors, she never looks directly at herself in them. (Image 2.7)

She fits in a sense into Cavell's category of 'melodramas of the unknown women',[13] although in this case, she is profoundly unknown not so much to others (Cavell's meaning) but to herself. The one time she does see herself, it is her reflection in the new TV screen and she sees in effect a vision of the future her children want to consign her to, the modern equivalent of walling the woman up with the dead husband. (Image 2.8)

---

[13]Stanley Cavell, *Contesting Tears*. I mean it conforms to Cavell's understanding in the following sense. As Cavell puts it, in some melodramas, the woman wants both to know, and that means that she seeks an education, senses there is something she must learn, and especially wants to be known, to be properly acknowledged as separate and independent in her own right. But Cary's inchoate desire to be educated anew in a way of life she is intrigued by and somewhat afraid of (a life in which she could freely realize her romantic desire) is frustrated. In this sense, Ron is a phony educator, partly because he plays the role of

Image 2.7

The effect of this first encounter is Cary's choice of a bright red dress to go to the country club party, a signal of a kind of sexual awakening that is lost on no one. Notice the red scarf on the daughter, as if she is announcing she is on the verge of being sexually active. In this scene we see as well an extraordinarily explicit acting out of Ned's Oedipal interest in his mother's sexuality. (Image 2.9)

I mention Kay and the scarf, because when she announces her own engagement, she announces her full awakening in an identical fashion (although she conforms to her brother's anxiety about low cut dresses). (Image 2.10)

---

educator so theatrically, and as if he does not need to be educated himself. (Although he inches toward such a realization by trying to fashion a home that Cary will understand and love, a home that can be for both of them.) He is not, though, the Thoreauvian hero he thinks he is, but a commercial tree farmer, and he is uncompromising and dogmatic (not that these traits are completely absent in Thoreau himself). He is not exempt, no one is, from the demands of a ruthless competitive capitalism. It, together with bank loans, competition with other farmers, crop failures, and so forth, is just off stage, as is so much of his life. So she is intrigued by a fantasy Ron has of himself, one that turns out to be a smug self-satisfied self-image.

Image 2.8

Image 2.9

The fact that Kay naively tries to explain to her mother the Oedipal complex, rather clumsily suggesting out loud that Ned desires his mother sexually and is jealous of Harvey as a rival, does not seem to be incidental. For the nature of Ron's interest in Cary, which is not clear on the surface, could easily be understood as itself Oedipal, a

Image 2.10

love for a mother figure, and so correspondingly, Cary's interest in Ron could be vaguely and at least symbolically incestuous. (It is striking that there is no mention at all in the film of Ron's mother. People compliment Ron on his father, but it is as if the mother never existed, and she may still be alive. Such an absence cannot be unrelated to his desire for Cary.)[14] This may have something to do with the town's anxiety about Cary and Ron. Their assumption seems to be that there is something 'unnatural' about their love, that something about the basic law that distinguishes and rules social order, the prohibition against incest, is at stake. (It is also quite striking that, while it would be obvious in 1955 that, given Cary's age,

---

[14]The only time we hear Ron express why he is attracted to Cary, it is in response to Cary's questioning why he and Mick had been looking at her and laughing when they first met. Ron tells her that he told Mick she had the finest pair of legs he has ever seen. (How would he know, in those dresses?) He is not in the slightest embarrassed at being caught in such locker-room banter with his friend, and Cary silently accepts the objectifying compliment, but it is clear that Sirk is making a point about Ron's relation to women.

there would be almost no chance of children, that issue never comes up, as if it is obvious both that children are out of the question and that Ron feels no qualms about what he is 'giving up'.)[15] Sirk also takes care to point out cinematically that this anxiety is not only irrational (there is no literal or even implicit actual incestuous desire, just a faint reminder of its prohibition), but strictly gendered as well. He inserts a small subplot in which an older man in Stoningham, Tom Allenby, is going to marry a woman young enough to be his daughter, a woman Sara calls 'that moron JoAnne', who 'bagged' Tom. In that case Sara, who has just been so censorious, is *throwing them a party*, the party at which the attempt to 'introduce' the class invader, Ron, fails so miserably.

The first act's emphasis on the banality and self-satisfaction of the country club set prepare us well for Cary's dive into romance, her escape. When they first of all kiss, however, we begin to notice (probably on a second or third viewing) something uncomfortable about Ron. The air of confidence and masculinity (of a sort) that clearly attracts Cary also borders on and sometimes falls into smugness and patronizing, another kind of policing of Cary. Ron appears to be smirking with self-satisfaction. And the bewildered expression on Cary's face also something we have seen and will see throughout, is telling. (Images 2.11 and 2.12)

Ron's smugness continues when they return home. When she tries to beg off seeing him again when he returns from a trip, we see him

---

[15]As with Oedipus, the prospect of generating children (having generated children) with one's mother is horrific to contemplate, subverts both the family and political life. It could be said to be an attempt to return to and to become one's own origin, the progenitor of oneself, in the ultimate act of autonomy, autochthony.

Image 2.11

Image 2.12

patronizingly insist that 'I'll see you,' again with the smirk. The fact that Rock Hudson is so huge compared to Jane Wyman helps sustain this rather ominous mood and in all their close scenes together, he looms over her, often with that smirk. And throughout, their embraces and kisses are, while intimate, oddly passionless, even a bit sexless.[16] (It cannot be incidental to making *Walden* a kind of intellectual touchstone in the film, that Thoreau's world is also sexless.) Cary doesn't smile much, always appears stunned and confused rather than liberated and happy.[17]

The contrast that Sirk stages between the two evening parties, a raucous celebration, full of genuine good feeling with Ron's friends, and the staid, quiet, gossipy and phony country club party and Sara's reception could not be clearer. (Images 2.13 and 2.14)

And, apart from the decidedly upper middle-class look of Mick's apartment and Alida's clothes, that contrast is subject to no ironic distancing. Cary is as genuinely happy at Ron's party as we ever see her, and there is no question that the film tilts sympathetically towards Ron and his friends and their Thoreauvian ideals.[18] But Cary's capacity to find happiness is not the same thing as *marrying* Ron, crossing lines of both class and sex conventions, marrying not only 'her gardener'

---

[16]It is true that it was somewhat of an open secret in Hollywood that Rock Hudson was gay, but it nevertheless remained, publicly, a secret and Hudson remained the biggest box office star of the period as a romantic leading man. I see no evidence that Sirk wanted to make any reference to Hudson's sexuality in the films in which he starred. And Hudson could be noticeably more passionate when directed to, as in *Magnificent Obsession*.

[17]Harvey, *Movie Love in the Fifties*, pp. 375–6. Note also Harvey's reports of Sirk's impatience with 'sentimentality', a trait that should surprise the early critics of his melodramas.

[18]There is an extremely subtle, almost invisible, indication of the persistence of class and ethnic lines being maintained in the group. When we see Cary introduced to Manuel and his family at this party, we see a lovely young girl, his daughter Marguerita. Cary, who has already been taken aback by the presence of what she takes to be an obvious and far too formidable rival, the Anderson's niece, Mary Ann, completely ignores Marguerita. But Sirk always keeps Marguerita in the background or at the edge of the frame in the party scenes, and clearly directs her to look glum, sullen and even angry throughout, presumably that the handsome bachelor Ron is ignoring her in favour of a much older woman. (She is the only one at the party who never smiles or gets into the swing of things.) It is as if she knows that a Latina woman could never have a chance with Ron (Mary Ann is always flirting with him) and Cary seems to take that for granted too.

Image 2.13

Image 2.14

but also someone much younger. Marrying Ron (as opposed especially to marrying Harvey) is like shouting to everyone that she is still capable of sexual desire and romantic attachment, and that she is (at least temporarily) willing to defy her censorious children and flaunt the town's puritanical conventions. But when Ron asks her to marry him, it is clear she has not thought that far ahead and when she does, she is terrified. Cary's reaction is predictably panicked, but she is also asking for help from Ron in imagining a new life, concerns about *her* that he is indifferent to, insisting simply that she can do whatever she wants to do. This is all the language of authenticity and genuineness in a life, as the Thoreauvian idea re-emerges, but she is making the plausible point that 'being herself' will also, must, carry along in its wake many other people, her children, her close friends. She seems to realize that there might be no compromise allowed between the bourgeois world and the art and nature- and artisan-oriented crowd she will join and that she will be 'turning her back on everything she knows'. Cary initially rejects the idea, goes to leave, breaks the Wedgewood teapot, as she breaks Ron's heart (the breakage seems to help her realize this),[19] weakens at the door, and they reconcile.

As they come closer to making their engagement public, Sirk makes a point about the gendered nature of the enforcement of class and sexual boundaries; that is, that the enforcement falls heavily on the woman, not the man, and that the very definition of genuineness that Ron imagines for himself is an option only for men. Ron continually asks her not to care about what people think, but it never seems to dawn on him that he gives no quarter in demanding that she think like him; in effect that it is 'my way or the highway'. It simply means, he says, 'being a man'. We see Cary hesitate and then accept the characterization, that being herself, Ron's great ideal, will mean

---

[19]Another subtle mark of the fate of their relationship: the precious teapot, which has been identified with Cary's world, is broken so badly that it can never be repaired. It would be a different film if the final scene had included a shot of it fully repaired.

'being a man', not at all being herself. (Earlier in the film, Cary had seemed to us as a woman with an ironic dimension, as when she says 'At least not in Egypt', and in the way she talks about Harvey. She seems now to be imitating Ron's self-seriousness, and Ron of course is totally without irony. This issue will return in the last section.)

We see this even more dramatically through the bourgeois toleration of a predatory male in their midst, Howard Moffer, who is guilty of far worse than marrying someone younger. (We are thereby also reminded that the town's reaction would very likely not occur, in fact does not occur, were the gender roles reversed. As noted earlier, the party at Sara's is in celebration of just such a December-May marriage.) He clearly assumes that Cary, by, in his eyes, trumpeting to the world that she is still interested in sex, has opened to door to him, and, drunk and disorderly, he ruins the reception at which Ron was supposed to have been introduced to Cary's world.

Cary's children turn out to be petulant, whining self-involved brats, who do what they can to express disgust at the prospect of their mother's marriage. Ron, like Howard, like everyone, assumes and has the gall to say to his own mother that she is interested only in a 'set of muscles', or that she is giving in to brute animal lust, and that if she goes through with it, he will never visit her again. (There is never a full reconciliation scene with them, and after bemoaning the loss of their familial home, they will later abandon it anyway and disappear from the film. They exit unredeemed and unredeemable.)[20]

---

[20]There is a feeble apology from Kay, when she announces her own marriage and seems to have some very dim awareness of how much pain she has caused her mother, but Cary reiterates that it is 'too late', and there is no warm reconciliation. The scene maintains a tonality of sadness.

Image 2.15

Finally, Cary succumbs to the pressure, and tries to convince Ron to wait, to move into her house and to live in her world. Ron refuses and we then see two firsts: Cary exercising some real independence and Ron losing that façade of self-confidence that had so often slipped into self-satisfaction. (Image 2.15) Their affair appears to be over.

The children return for Christmas (their condition having been met), and everything has changed. They pressured their mother to give up her fiancé, but then, it turns out, they are moving away and urge Cary to sell the very house Ned had proclaimed so sacred to the family tradition. And they buy her a TV set so she won't be lonely, perhaps the bitterest irony in a film full of irony. It is clearly the modern version of walling the widow up in the tomb.

What emerges at the end of the film as their reconciliation scene (and another of those problematic happy endings) is prepared for by two scenes that are telling. In Ron's case, we return to a reminder about gender and power in both worlds, Ron's and Cary's, and in

Cary's, as noted, her initiative is a matter of health, as 'prescribed' by her doctor. In Ron's, the jocular Mick tells Ron that women do not want to make up their own mind; they want the man to make up their minds for them (so much for 'to thine own self be true'), and he encourages Ron to do so.

And her doctor tells Cary, insightfully, that she was ready for a love affair, not love. And we see that much of Cary's hesitation has had to do with her anxiety about being older. She has been secretly worried since Mick's party that Alida's blonde, young, attractive cousin would be hard for Ron to resist and that he must have taken up with her. When she finds out the cousin is marrying someone else, her inner hesitation is resolved and she drives out to the mill, but again her resolve falters and she drives away without knocking. Ron sees this and tries to call out to her, but loses his footing and suffers a bad fall, is seriously injured. As noted earlier, given that she turns away from door, it is crucial that any reconciliation seems therefore to *require* Ron's fall and injury. So Ron is running somewhat recklessly toward Cary just as she is deliberately turning away from any possible reconciliation. His desperate attempt to reach her and then his fall and injury suggest, very briefly, a dimension to Ron we had not seen before, given his self-satisfaction and patronizing attitude. He can certainly be injured, hurt by Cary, and his bravado seems now more a protective device than genuine. At any rate, this all sets up the final scene in the film.

Several things are visually important in the last scene. First the mill has been made over to look like what James Harvey has called an extreme version of *Better Homes and Gardens*, Cary's world, only glossier and pushed 'to almost lunatic extremes of elaboration and rich

Image 2.16

deadness – in colour'.[21] The second is that the familiar visual geometry of Ron looming over Cary is reversed, as Cary is now overlooking him, injured, broken in effect and in bed, passive. (Image 2.16)

It is very tempting to think that this reversal represents not only what makes possible the reconciliation (that Cary now has the 'upper' hand, with the injured Ron 'diminished') but that their future will now *maintain* such a relationship. Their new world will still have upper middle-class types like Mick and Alida in it, and the redecorating of the mill means a reduplication of Cary's old world, with some idea of their own authenticity projected on it all. The romance had begun in autumn and is now resolved in some way or other in the dead of winter. This either presages that spring will soon arrive, or that the lack of warmth and the somewhat fraught sexual passion we had seen

---

[21]Harvey, *Movie Love in the Fifties*, p. 374. As noted earlier, this is a little extreme. Ron had been content in his greenhouse, and he is clearly trying to appoint the new space with taste, in some sense a tastefulness he thinks Cary should recognize. And she does recognize that it was all made over 'with love'.

in their scenes together simply and finally figures their romantic fate together. All the signs point to the latter. And the deer we had seen before returns. Previously it had seemed to figure Ron's 'nourishing' Cary's need for love, her dependence on him, but now it seems not to figure Cary's dependence on Ron, but the reverse, and somehow Sirk has managed to have the deer seem confused and stunned a bit, as if to remind us that Ron has no idea what he is in for, will be in the same state for some time.[22] Nothing we have seen suggests that the town will change, or even that Cary will change very much. What looks like the reunion of two now independent, self-reliant souls is simply one more way of compromising with the requirements of bourgeois life. Ron has been diminished in power and authority, will continue to turn trees into commodities, and Cary, we expect, will manage to find a way, most likely through self-deceit, to imagine that what they do together will be authentic and their own, even as it reproduces the norms that we have seen enforced throughout.

Much of the dialogue and Ron's injury itself seem tinged with irony. The doctor, in telling Cary that Ron's recovery will take time, that he will need her help, that it will last a while, seems just as much to be describing what Ron will face in hitching himself to a well-

---

[22]Harvey notes that the deer seems trapped between the picture window and the painted landscape behind it. *Movie Love in the Fifties*, p. 376. T. Schatz also notes the irony that the 'alternate' lifestyle of Mick and Alida (apparently the model for Ron's renovation) is hardly a departure from Cary's upper middle-class style. *Hollywood Genres: Formulas. Filmmaking and the Studio System* (New York: Random House, 1981), p. 251. One might also add that the notion of the deer trapped could parallel the different way nature is manifest after picture windows became part of American architecture: framed, almost posed, and hardly any longer nature as it meant to Thoreau. And even in Thoreau, once nature *is taken up* as significant and 'for us', it is already no longer mere nature. This parallels the authenticity point made here. I am indebted to Tom Gunning for a discussion about this issue.

meaning but still very conventional woman, how much 'help' he will need in getting over his 'injury', recovering from his 'broken' status. (This 'needing help' scene mirrors an earlier one after the proposal when Ron also pleads that he will need help adjusting.) If they are to reunite, it will at least at the outset be with Cary in a conventional role, nurse and mother. What will happen when Ron is well is left unclear. Cary had been persuaded and perhaps a bit intimidated by Ron into marrying him; she had been bullied out of marrying him by her children; she had been embarrassed into reconciling with him by the doctor, only to fail at the last minute, and she is now moved by concern and pity to nurse him back to health, but we sense no fundamental transformation or new resolve. There is nothing left of her 'red dress' announcement of sexual desire and availability, something that may make their relationship much more acceptable in town.[23] And Ron, of course, cannot act on Mick's advice either, 'to make up Cary's mind for her'. All he could do to bring this about was fall off a cliff. This kind of stalemate is what we should expect given Sirk's sentiments about the American bourgeoisie, that their 'homes are prisons', and that 'they are imprisoned even by the tastes of the society in which they live'.[24] In the final scene, we note at the very end the effect of the deer as a near perfect embodiment of Sirk's unique version of cinematic irony. Somehow the poor, confused deer figures for us what has become of the self-consciously virile, 'my way or the highway' Ron. (Image 2.17)

---

[23]See Mulvey's apposite summation of where Cary finds herself in 'Notes on Sirk and Melodrama', p. 79.
[24]'Interview with Douglas Sirk', p. 32. Quoted in Schatz, *Hollywood Genres*, p. 253

Image 2.17

The film ends, leaving us with two general issues raised. I mentioned at the beginning that the film establishes some sort of connection between the anxious policing of class boundaries and the policing of sexual conventions. By the enforcing of such conformism, I mean to refer to a conformism familiar in nineteenth- and twentieth-century fiction. One could call it 'Girardian'.[25] In the absence of any substantive common value, we anxiously watch each other for signs of what is worth wanting, and take some comfort in following the lead of 'most people', or 'most people in our social class' for signs of what ought to be done, or to be thought or to be desired. If we were to question that, we would be in uncharted waters, a source of great anxiety because we sense we would have lost all standards. (As Girard points out, this reliance on others also provokes a great resentment against them, since the reliance comes with the realization that they are no better

---

[25]René Girard, *Deceit, Desire, and the Novel: Self and Other in Literary Structure*, transl. Y. Freccero (Baltimore: The Johns Hopkins University press, 1961). See especially the first chapter, 'Triangular Desire', pp. 1–52. This structure might just as well be called Hegelian.

than I am, do not deserve the authority I feel compelled to grant them.) Another aspect of the general anxiety is obvious. While class differences rest on real inequality, on money and the access to power that they provide, the idea of class as a kind of exclusionary norm, or the idea that members of it are therewith entitled to live a different life, exists as such only in being asserted and acknowledged and internalized, especially by those who are excluded. (Once it is successfully internalized it can paradoxically become almost invisible, as evinced by the infrequency of its invocation in American political discourse.) Sustaining it requires the policing of perception and desire as well as the maintenance of real material power. So it is one thing to have a fling with your gardener, which Mona and the other town gossips vicariously believe for a while Cary is doing, seeming to take some pleasure in the spectacle. It is another to attempt to ignore a class boundary and so class privilege for the sake of love, to establish legally a precedent or model that others could follow. Cary is thus directly challenging the idea that class is a mark of some significant differentiator in human life, and by acting as she does she treats it as the fantasy it is. Class in this latter sense, as an entitlement to special privilege and a requirement to marry your 'kind', is in itself 'nothing' at all, nothing real. (It has as much 'reality' as the belief that the blood of aristocrats is distinctive.) Cary is on the verge of exposing that and so stands as a potential 'traitor to her class'.

That said, it must also be said that the film does not treat the role of class in the lives of these characters as dispensable. The symbolic role of class, its public, theatrical dimension, is clearly a major source of the self-worth of the country club set; perhaps, together with wealth, the only source of standing or self-respect available in the town. If a gardener is 'as good as' a country club member, then any claim to elevated status is exposed as the fantasy it is. And everything and everyone in the film works hard to maintain that fantasy, however destructive it is to any ideal of integrity or authenticity. And to a large extent they succeed. The 'home' that Ron has built for Cary is Cary's home; indeed, her world.

Cary's ultimate timidity and apparent inability to place herself outside the conventions she has known and accepted all her life, and Ron's self-congratulatory sense of autonomy and nonconformist rigidity descend from an American social imaginary dealt with in all Sirk's great melodramas and represent contrasting poles of the dialectic of dependence and independence that that imaginary requires. Such a tension would understandably make any deviation from marriage norms fraught with anxiety and confusion. Ron can maintain his sense of himself only by drawing Cary wholly into his world, and Cary can keep her relations with her friends and family, not to mention her Wedgewood china, three strings of pearls, country club and mink coat tastes, only by somehow or other pulling Ron into her orbit, and that is possible only after Ron has 'fallen'.[26] Or, in another version of a dialectic that can become a paradox, the bourgeois marriage understands itself as a product of passionate romantic love, but can only be properly realized by contract and an impossible legal promise to love. But who writes the contract?

---

[26]It is difficult to imagine a social life for the two that could combine both the country club crowd and the Mick-Alida community. Dinner parties with Sara, or Mona at Mick's place are hard to picture. It might be tempting to see some possibility as even conceivable because Ron has in effect *sacrificed* himself for Cary, that his broken state is something he is willing to do for her. But he actually does nothing; he stumbles and falls accidentally. One can imagine him coming out of his concussion and returning to the Ron we saw in their breakup scene.

A final general theme is that issue of authenticity, Ron's 'answer', his guiding lode star. In the conformist world of Stoningham, perhaps of America in general, it is certainly understandable that such genuineness would emerge as some sort of virtue. And for many philosophers, starting with Rousseau and Diderot, and extending through Kierkegaard, Tocqueville, Nietzsche, Heidegger and Sartre, it is treated as a kind of new master virtue, the trait of character that is the most crucial in the emerging modern mass-consumer societies.

But the first problem with Ron's self-conscious embodiment of such an ideal is evident in his air of smug self-satisfaction and in his 'be a man' homily. For, to invoke a familiar figure for such a notion, one assumes that one has 'found' oneself and now must find a way of remaining true to what one has found. But the philosophical treatments of the ideal in Kierkegaard, Nietzsche, Heidegger, and in Emerson and Thoreau (as interpreted by Cavell), the emphasis is on the enormous *difficulty* of any such 'finding'. The intricacies of social dependence in modern, mass-consumer societies, the near feudal power of managers in corporate empires, and a heightened awareness of the difference between public personae and private attitudes, make any settled sense of just 'being' oneself immediately naïve. (Compare Kierkegaard's sense that in the modern age the only true Christians are those who cannot be Christians and know they cannot be.) Or, any such sense ought to inspire a different sort of scepticism than about the external world or other minds, but about one's sense of oneself. This would be the kind of irony mentioned earlier here, a kind of ethical stance. As in Cavell's treatment, this is not a scepticism that demands or intimates a 'solution', as if a philosophical problem, but a fate to be borne. And bearing it cannot be a matter of resigning oneself to an inevitable self-deceit (as in typified in Sartre on bad faith), or to a kind of cynical playfulness, but simply a lived-out realization of the great difficulty (not the impossibility) of any 'finding' and 'being' who one 'genuinely' is. There is no model or principle to guide any such recovered life. Any such picture or formulation would be subject to infinite qualifications and endless nuances. But there are characters in novels and films who have arrived somewhere, found something, reached some state of mind that can at least be suggestive, provide some sort of illumination. Or the absence of such characters (and there are none in Sirk's Universal melodramas) can also imply something determinate about what is missing or still hidden, forgotten.[27]

It is important, too, that we are shown that the naïveté of Ron's sense of what authenticity requires is linked to his constant avoidance of the dialectic of dependence and independence that is often raised by the film's point of view, by what our attention is directed to. His sense of himself is self-certifying, closed to any sense of how he seems to others, a sense that might have awakened him to the difficulty he is simplifying. Cary must think for herself as long as she thinks like him, about marriage, where to live, and what friends to have. He is in effect 'broken' by her refusal to do so, but we sense he is likely to think of it all as a compromise, even a sacrifice of himself for her, and that too is self-congratulatory rather than genuinely reflective. What he never realizes is that authenticity is a cooperative or a social virtue.

---

[27]Cavell's examples of re-marriages in *Pursuits of Happiness* would be a good place to start, especially with Jean, Barbara Stanwyck's character in *The Lady Eve* (1941), at the end of her journey from con artist to genuine lover.

Finally, the idea of authenticity as some sort of *goal to be sought* can easily seem paradoxical, as it does in this film, with Ron wavering between dogmatic and smug self-assertion, and broken submission, as if 'true' to a new, but now dependent self that he will never be able to acknowledge as such. This whole situation can be greatly compounded by self-deceit; one knows that one is not able to, not allowed to, represent oneself as who one is, but can manage, over even a lifetime, to hide that somehow from oneself. (Most audiences, I think, accept this temptation in Sirk's films.)

Put another way, the more authenticity, or the avoidance of such self-deceit, needed, as modern mass-consumer societies took shape, to be praised as a virtue, the more suspicious its expression became (that is, just as it became part of a conscious social *strategy*). Once it became publicly acknowledged as a virtue or even as significant, it became suspicious, a strategic means, if only to self-congratulation, as is the case with Ron. *Being* authentic is one thing; *trying to be* and especially *trying to be seen* as authentic immediately borders on the theatrical.[28]

No aspect of this way of looking at what Sirk's film shows us should be understood as a *moral* critique of Ron's smugness or Cary's fear. The ambiguous and somewhat ominous fate of Ron's and Cary's love affair, perhaps of the fate of love itself in such a world, is nowhere treated by Sirk as the failure of individuals to live up to their own convictions or to have the courage to risk ostracism and gossip. Any

---

[28]Ron has his own philosophy, formulates it explicitly and is thought of by others as embodying this expressed philosophy. He is also willing to lecture people solemnly about its tenets. His standing as a character would be much different if Ron were played by, say, Gary Cooper in his prime; laconic, a man of few or no words, simply *being* himself. See also Lionel Trilling, *Sincerity and Authenticity* (Cambridge: Harvard University Press, 1973) for similar Hegelian points.

aspiration to the intimacy, vulnerability and deep reciprocity of love and friendship can come to mean what it does to the agents, can come to require what it does, can run the enormous risks it does, only in a specific social and historical world, and in the world Sirk shows us, the American modern bourgeois world in the immediate postwar years, there is not much hope that such aspirations can ever be realized.

There is one last philosophical dimension to Sirkian irony that is worth mentioning. That the world of Stoningham is treated ironically simply means at a first level that we are shown that things are not as they seem, either to the viewers of the film (most viewers, I suspect), or, especially, to the inhabitants, the players of the theatrical social game of status seeking and boundary policing. Their moral judgements are staged strategies of self-serving protectiveness. That can seem obvious, but it can appear to be the singular traits of self-involved, thoughtless people, and that is not what it seems. But there is yet another level to the irony. Since the irony is not destructive or cynical we are also being called on to attend to what it would be to live without such theatricality and falseness. And part of what a philosophical reading of a film, one attentive to this difference and to the generality of the problem, can accomplish is to call to mind, however indistinctly at first, whatever is missing in the lives we see – call it mutuality, reciprocity and respect, love, socially realized freedom, genuineness or, following Cavell, 'the ordinary'.[29] In Cavell's treatments, what is hidden,

---

[29]The theme is of course everywhere in Cavell, but I am thinking here of the special bearing on this film of *This New Yet Unapproachable America* and *Conditions Handsome and Unhandsome: The Constitution of Emersonian Perfectionism* (Chicago: University of Chicago Press, 1991), and more generally in *The Claim of Reason: Wittgenstein, Skepticism, Morality, and Tragedy* (Oxford: Oxford University Press, 1999).

very hard to recover, is so because layered over with ossified habits of mind, with too much taken for granted, habits that make it hard even to notice that anything might be missing. In a fine phrase, he once called what is missing an 'intimacy lost'.[30] (Hegel would call the goal of such proper, corrective attending 'the actual', or 'the concrete'; also, he thinks, lost in the world he saw coming into being.) The attention to class differences and the role of gender and age policing in the community are treated in the film as the most important sources of the distortion, the ossified and unreflective habits of mind, the loss of what would otherwise be possible, what the intense aspiration to love, understood as a kind of inchoate resistance, aspires to. As noted, class is treated in the film as a cultural and social norm, and Sirk keeps the material sources of class power markedly hidden, as hidden and undiscussed as they tend to be in modern American life. Aside from Ron and Mick, no one ever talks about what they do in the male world of New York that every professional man in the town gets on a train to attend to every morning. Sirk's orientation is certainly focused on the real interests of the socially and economically powerful, but those interests are treated in their social and especially psychological manifestations; in snobbery, the jealous guarding of privilege, anxiety about the fragility of such privilege. Characters like Mona Plash, and what she and her friends represent, are at home in Sirk just as they would be in the novels of James and Proust, rather than in the context of a Dreiser novel (or in Stevens's cinematic treatment, *A Place in the Sun*), or in films by, say, Elia Kazan. At least Sirk's radical leftist past in Germany, his obvious fascination with the nature of these distortions

---

[30]S. Cavell, 'Politics as Opposed to What', in *Critical Inquiry* 9 (September 1982), p. 161.

and fantasies in the American experience, and of course the details of the film in question, make it reasonable to attribute to him such a concern in these terms. Given the hiddenness mentioned above, this treatment hardly gives us the full picture of class, power and the consequences of such a social order on the intimacies of daily life, but his treatment allows him, along with directors like Nicholas Ray, Max Ophuls and Alfred Hitchcock and a few others, to produce something distinctive in Hollywood commercial film – a politics of American emotional life.

None of this is even available for any reflection, however, if the ending of the film does not produce something of the unease we discussed in the last chapter. There is certainly genuine tenderness and concern in Cary's attitude and what seems a resolve to stick it out with Ron in the future. She will stay with him. But we remember that she turned away from his door, that this new bond with Ron was not of her making. And there is an airlessness, even a sort of deadness in the tonality of the scene, not to mention that we are left with a final image, bordering on the comically ironic, of the bewildered deer, as if an avatar for both Cary and the viewers, unable fully to take in this result. Cary and we must make do with the fact that this is 'all that heaven allows' and as Sirk in his own voice reminds us, 'heaven is stingy'.

3

Misplaced Moralism in *Written on the Wind*

Written on the Wind (1956) is both a family and a romantic melodrama and any summary of its plot will remind one of soap operas, and that of course will make it immediately difficult for many to take the film seriously. The family is a billionaire oil dynasty, the Hadleys. It consists of an ageing, dying patriarch, Jaspar Hadley (played by Jaspar Keith), his two spoiled, self-indulgent children, Kyle, an alcoholic playboy (played by Robert Stack) and the sexually promiscuous Marylee Hadley (played by Dorothy Malone). Kyle's boyhood friend, scandal-fixer, and chief geologist for the company is Mitch Wayne (played by Rock Hudson), and the main cast is completed by an elegant New York advertising executive, Lucy Moore (played by Lauren Bacall), who becomes Mrs Kyle Hadley early in the film. Marylee Hadley is desperately in love with Mitch, who does not return the love, and regards Marylee, he says, as more of a sister. After a whirlwind one day romance, Lucy and Kyle marry, but trouble soon develops when Kyle learns that there is a problem with his fertility, which he regards as a devastating blow to his manhood, and he returns to heavy drinking. Mitch has in the meantime fallen for Kyle's wife, Lucy, and finally declares his love for her, but she remains at least technically faithful to Kyle. Marylee, jealous that Mitch loves Lucy, not her, falsely tells Kyle that Lucy and Mitch are having an affair, and when Kyle learns that Lucy is pregnant, believing the child is Mitch's (it isn't) explodes in anger, beats Lucy, is thrown out by Mitch. He returns for the violent conclusion, when he is shot in a struggle for a gun. Marylee, who had vowed to say out of spite that Mitch killed Kyle, relents at the trial, tells the truth, and is left alone in the mansion as Mitch and Lucy drive off in what appears to be one of those happy endings.

One can see the difference between the banality of the plot details and the ambition of the directorial style from the opening scene, which suggests a grandeur and epic sweep to what would appear to be an obvious cliché of unhappy, entitled rich people and their damaging impact on ordinary people. The beginning of the film starts near the end of the story, with Kyle Hadley's death. (Such a technique in a film or novel suggests immediately a fatalism in the narrative. What will happen has already happened and there is nothing the characters can do about it.) Everything about the opening suggests a mythic picture of the country America has become. First an ugly, ominous, inhuman industrial landscape in a country fuelled by oil, the American narcotic that was the basis of the Rockefeller, Getty and so many Texas fortunes. (Image 3.1)

Since the Hadleys represent a very powerful image of success in the American imaginary, vast wealth and power, beginning the film this way will also suggest the spiritual devastation and emptiness, ugliness, of the life we are about to see depicted. Then there is the confusion of public and private, with the Hadley name so prominently displayed

Image 3.1

that it suggests what we will learn is the reality: the town is virtually a feudal estate of the Hadleys. Vast amounts of money have created in America a new aristocracy like this one, but a vulgar, materialistic, narcissistic elite. Then there is the emphasis on speed and recklessness as Kyle careens through the town in his yellow sports car, as well as self-indulgence and carelessness. The way the opening is framed contributes to a sense that this whole way of life, not just Kyle, is heading towards some catastrophe. And finally the ironic image of contrasts, the vulgar expensive yellow car, Kyle's toy (what Marylee calls his 'kiddie car'),[1] contrasted with the classic pillars of the plantation style, a pathetic and false attempt at old-world elegance. (Image 3.2)

But then, in a perfect realization of the double nature of Sirk's films, melodrama and meta-melodrama at the same time, the ominous and ugly tonality shifts to sentimentality and a vague self-pity. (There is a

---

[1] *Witten on the Wind* (1956, Universal), directed by Douglas Sirk; screenplay by George Zuckerman from a story by Robert Wilder. All screengrabs from this film were made by me.

Image 3.2

clever and continuous transition in the musical theme from ominous
and epic to romantic and regretful, with the latter a clear variation
on the former.) We are introduced to the main characters in highly
stylized visual vignettes; Mitch occupies the position of Kyle, the
husband, in his bedroom with Lucy in bed, looking down on Kyle
from his position of moral superiority; we see Lucy, weakened by her
beating and miscarriage; then the scheming Marylee inserting herself
into the scene, and the drunken Kyle stumbling toward what will be
his death. A strong wind blows autumn leaves through the opened
door, creating the odd impression that the house is abandoned. With
the shift in tonality and atmosphere the theme song of the film sung
by The Four Aces in a recognizable 1950s ballad style, the details of
which audiences for the most part ignore, begins to suggest another,
stranger psychological dimension to the film.

The song seems to tell a tale of adultery. 'A faithless lover's kiss is
written on the wind; A night of stolen bliss is written on the wind';

and 'The promises we made are whispers in the breeze; They echo and they fade just like our memories.'[2] This is the first sign of the film's ironic complexity. The song we are listening to tells the tale of infidelity, of a faithless lover, and it expresses a very pessimistic view of romantic love, its promises treated as mere writings in the wind, evanescent, untrustworthy. But there is no faithless lover in the film. Kyle has not committed adultery, but he has been manipulated into believing that Mitch and Lucy have, so the song might be said to express his anxiety as he drives home. So we begin with a very dark picture of an alcoholic and violent Kyle, the song oddly expressing his point of view (if anyone in the film would believe in the weakness of romantic promises, regardless of the truth, it is Kyle), even though its role as a theme song also announces that that point of view seems to be the film's and does so with a sympathy for Kyle boarding on the maudlin. (We should also reserve judgement about whether the accusation in the song, that there has been a faithless love, is in some sense true. It would not be right to say that Mitch and Lucy have been 'faithful' to Kyle in some fuller sense of loyalty and solidarity.) But again, what is unusual is that this dimension of the film is largely if not completely unnoticed by most audiences, and this for a reason that is formally and stylistically suggested by the film itself.

That is, melodramas are made from the point of view of the modern bourgeoisie for bourgeois audiences. Sirk can thus rely on a predictable moralization of what we will see. That is, he can rely on audiences'

---

[2]The film's title and song title derive from Robert Wilder's 1945 novel. Peter William Evans reports in *Written on the Wind* (London: Palgrave McMillan, 2013) that the sentiment – that a woman's promises in particular 'should be written in wind and running water' – can be traced back to Catullus, p. 11.

distaste with what they will see as the opulence, corruption, even depravity of Kyle and Marylee, at the fact that their vast wealth is just a vehicle for selfish self-indulgence, and he can count on an audience identification with Mitch and Lucy as the 'good people', who actually work for a living, caught up in the Hadley corruption and fighting their way out of it, snared by chance in a tragic love that they righteously struggle against consummating. The two of them are as much spectators of the ugly Hadley circus as the movie audience and this identification will provide the richest source of irony. The irony is that just suggested. Although Kyle's view of his wife and friend's faithlessness is false, at another level, a level that strikes against the audience as well, Kyle is onto something. This begins in the subtlest of way, with the theme song suggesting an indictment of Mitch and Lucy for faithlessness, and so, since Sirk can count on the audience not sharing that view, and their regarding Mitch and Lucy as the hero and heroine of the film, Kyle and Marlyee the villains, in that way he also begins to imply an indictment of the audience for their thoughtless identification with these representatives of what is supposed to be bourgeois rectitude. Even what appear to be direct, even primal emotional responses to narrated events would thus also reflect the stake the audience and the couple have in such bourgeois rectitude and the sense of status and superiority that such an investment provides. It provides them with the same sort of source for a community standing, self-worth and respectability that social class does in *All That Heaven Allows*, that fame will in *Imitation of Life* in the next chapter. The melodramatic caricatures in these opening visual vignettes, their clearly overdone quality, are as much a comment on the audience's need for the staples of melodrama morality, as it is an indulgence and satisfaction of that need.

Of course, not all of this can be derived from the opening song alone, not to mention what Sirk might be trying to say about the emotional logic of American melodrama, but it is a beginning. We will need some more details to see how this develops. The film can be loosely organized in five different chapters. There is first the whirlwind romance between Lucy and Kyle. Second, there is the first phase of their marriage, which appears stable. Throughout all the chapters, there are two continuous sublots. One is the psychological effect of a 'Texas' assumption about masculinity. The patriarch, Jaspar, is clearly disappointed that his son Kyle is not more like Mitch, not more connected with the hunting, rural, cowboy culture that is represented by Mitch and his father, an old friend of Jaspar's. And there is no question that Kyle knows this and has had to live with it every day of his life. Mitch has been raised as Kyle's constant companion, and in effect his baby-sitter in early adulthood, even to the point of taking the blame for some of Kyle's misbehaviour. (This fact is more extraordinary than it might appear on a first viewing. It turns out that Mitch's father had essentially given Mitch away to the Hadley family to be raised in their home. We later see Mitch's boyhood room in the mansion. Since Mitch went to the same schools as Kyle and had many of the same advantages, one can imagine his father thinking this was all worth it, but what kind of a father would do this? And how resentful must Mitch have been, having no real claim on the family, and living with the expectation that he must always clean up after Kyle?) There is certainly no question that Mitch resents Kyle because of this, and although the surface of the film encourages us to admire Mitch just as Jaspar does, it will turn out that Mitch is quite the false friend, and acts out that resentment by continuously complaining about, whining about, Kyle. (He starts in on Mitch almost immediately in the film, in the cab taking Lucy to her first meeting with Kyle.) The other constant subplot is Marylee's desperate desire to be loved by Mitch and her increasing rage that he won't at the very least sleep with her. The third chapter begins Kyle's downward spiral as he learns that, while he is not infertile, he and Lucy will have unusual difficulties conceiving a child. This exacerbates Kyle's inferiority complex and he begins to drink heavily again. When Marylee suggests that Lucy and Mitch are having an affair, he believes her and when he discovers that Lucy is pregnant he is convinced he cannot be the father and that Mitch is. In the fourth chapter, this leads to the confrontation that ends with Kyle's death. The last chapter is the inquest into the death and the supposed happy ending, with Mitch and Lucy driving off and leaving Marylee alone, in control of the Hadley estate and its vast fortune.

Consider first the scene in which we are introduced, first to Mitch and Lucy and then Kyle. The rivalry between Kyle and Mitch begins immediately. Mitch had met Lucy first and invites her to a lunch he must attend with Kyle, who immediately ignores the fact that Lucy is Mitch's guest and crudely appropriates her for himself as if Mitch is not there. The first meeting between Mitch and Lucy, a secretary to an advertising director at Hadley Industries, is very typical of how Sirk inserts a great deal of usually unnoticed visual information in every scene. This is our first look at Lucy. (Image 3.3)

This is Lucy's world, New York, urban, sophisticated; an independent career woman, all miles away culturally from the town of Hadley, all of which makes her willingness to leave this world and her career harder to understand and, eventually, suspicious. Moreover, we see that her job is presenting a colourful face for Hadley Industries, and that

Image 3.3

there are a variety of different images she can choose, as if only the appearances matter, not the reality of the Hadley world, the colourless ugliness of which we have just seen.

When Rock Hudson's Mitch shows up, we also see a sign of Sirk's ambition. He frames Mitch next to a faux Joan Miró; not, I think a mere decorative touch, but a signal not only of Lucy's taste and sophistication but that we should take as seriously the visual details of his film as we should a Miró. (Image 3.4)

We don't really begin to notice until the end of the film that Mitch is a bitter and self-pitying man (not to mention passionless, wooden; one of his critics would call him a human tree trunk), constantly complaining about Kyle and the necessity for him to pick up after him. Nor does it immediately occur to us that, if he feels this way, he could simply leave. He is a top geologist and can apparently generate job offers at will, as he does later in the film. We also do not appreciate the quite cold and ambitious, designing nature of Lucy; all of this

Image 3.4

again because they are both the supposedly good people in melodramas, the hard-working, not privileged bourgeoisie. This is another example of an ironic undercurrent: Mitch and Lucy have either contempt or condescending pity for Kyle, feel superior to him, but they both have built and will build their lives on him and his wealth. We are not of course ready to conclude anything of any generality about the inevitability of such blindness in bourgeois moralism, but we are in early stages of what will be a sort of suggestion. Mitch, for example, after having endured the humiliation of having Kyle push him aside and begin trying to seduce Lucy, takes solace by estimating that Lucy, at least, is not like all the other women whom Kyle can conquer by dazzling them with his wealth. But it doesn't take much for Kyle to get Lucy into his private plane and to fly her to Miami, where the extent of what his wealth makes possible is on extraordinary display. There is a smugly confident expression on Mitch's face (confident that Lucy will find this all as vulgar as he does) as they enter the hotel room in Miami that Kyle has had stocked with

Image 3.5

every imaginable piece of clothing and accessories. Yet again, it is Sirk's style that conveys much of the meaning of the scene. The contrast between the drab greys and browns of their bourgeois business uniforms and the spectacular colours of the room begins to create some sympathy for any ordinary person dazzled by such a display, and even more interestingly it is a scene designed by Kyle (as well as Sirk). His tastes are as 'melodramatic' as Sirk's; excessive, theatrical, and, in psychological terms, such taste suggests a hint of desperation and insecurity on Kyle's part, not at all irony or self-consciousness. Like so many in this world, his status depends on his having bought whatever standing he has, so he might as well make great use of it.[3] (Images 3.5 and 3.6)

---

[3]Sirk said about the colour palette of the film: ' The whole picture is a kind of poster-style, with a flat, simple lighting that concentrates the effects. It's a kind of expressionism, of course like Wedekind or the late Strindberg, or the early Brecht. And I avoid what a painter might call the sentimental colours – pale or soft colours. Here I paint in primary colours, like Kirchner or Nolde for example.' Harvey, 'Sirkumstanial Evidence', *Film Comment*, (1978) 14, no. 4, p. 56.

Image 3.6

In a moment of cold reflection, for reasons we do not hear, Lucy decides to return to New York. But Kyle follows her to the airport and in just a few minutes, convinces her, not just to return to Miami, but, in a scene notable for its lack of romantic passion, to marry him. Lucy appears to be accepting a business proposal, but in a way that is likely to be quickly unnoticed. They do not have a family wedding (his father and sister meet her only after the wedding), and we hear Mitch's disappointment with Lucy when a reporter questions him about the wedding. ('Who is Lucy Moore?' 'It's a good question.' 'You mean you don't know her?' 'Not very well.')

When they return and a brief period of stability occurs in what I am calling the third chapter, the subplots concerning the patriarch and Marylee are more prominent. Jasper Hadley is not, as one might expect, a tyrannical paterfamilias; just the opposite. He is indecisive, weak and indulgent. He has produced an alcoholic son and a promiscuous self-demeaning daughter because he wants them to live up to some ideal he sees in Mitch, an ideal he associated with Mitch's father, a legendary hunter and rancher, and this is all an important aspect of the fantasy dimension of the American imaginary in general: the supposed honesty and integrity of the self-reliant rural life, essentially the old, independent, sometimes lawless frontier America. Such a contrast between supposedly real people and the phoniness of the urban sophisticates has a long history in the United States and has recently had some rather disastrous political consequences, and it shows up elsewhere in Sirk's films – in the appeal to Thoreau's *Walden* in his *All That Heaven Allows*, and Willa Cather's *My Antonia* in his *Tarnished Angels*. In all cases, as in this film, its destructiveness as a fantasy is on full view, as is the desperate need for the fantasy, the unsatisfying norms for manliness and the limited economic and class standards for self-respect in the modern world that provoke so much dissatisfaction.

Marylee's role is also further defined. She not only does not conform to moral codes and publicly flaunts herself in defiance, having one night stands with disreputable men and flaunting her sexuality, but she is a threat both to patriarchy (her promiscuity threatens the clarity of family inheritance) and capitalism, which at this point depended on a strict gender-based division of labour and so a domestic, powerless role for women.[4] (Image 3.7)

And as with Jaspar and Kyle and Mitch, part of her problem has to do with a fantasy of pre-civilized innocence, associated in the film with childhood and nature. She keeps returning to the river where she

---

[4]See C. Orr, 'Closure and Containment: Marylee Hadley in *Written on the Wind*', *Wide Angle* (1980), 4.2, p.31.

Image 3.7

played with Mitch, believing in effect that she is another person, that she can be another person, who dresses differently and acts differently, as if that is the real Marylee. (Image 3.8)

(The critic Thomas Elsaesser puts this whole situation well when he says that Marylee wants Mitch who wants Lucy who wants Kyle who just wants to die.)[5] It is obviously also the case that Sirk is well aware that these fantasies are also American film fantasies in Westerns, Frank Capra's or Howard Hawks's populist comedies, and in the mythology created around actors like Gary Cooper and John Wayne.

I should also mention that Sirk's desire to pack his films with visual information will also include visual jokes and puns. For example there is the scene in which Mitch is explaining to Marylee that he only loves her like a sister, that he has no passionate feelings for her or she

---

[5] T. Elsaesser, 'Tales of Sound and Fury', in *Home is Where the Heart Is: Studies in Melodrama and the Woman's Film*, ed. C. Gledhill (London: BFI, 1987), p. 64.

Image 3.8

Image 3.9

Image 3.10

'lights no fire' in him, all as he continually tries and fails to light a cigarette.[6] Or, when Marylee enters Mitch's old room, Sirk is not above positioning him and the ukulele in an obvious way. (Image 3.9)

I understand these as both reminders by Sirk to attentive viewers to pay attention to visual details, and signs that he is making, in effect, another movie at the same time as the Hollywood vehicle he was assigned. For example, an inattentive viewer will simply take for granted that Lucy simply fell in love with Kyle in one night and married him for that reason, however implausible that is. But we have already noted the lack of passion in their encounters and Sirk makes visual suggestions about the basis of her attraction, concentrating especially on jewellery. (Image 3.10)

---

[6]No doubt Mitch's resistance to Marylee does not have to do with his sibling bond. Marrying her would be to render permanent his public dependence on the largesse of the Hadley's and would be, in his frontier code, unmanly (whereas a woman, 'marrying up', suffers no such stigma). See the discussion in Orr, 'Closure', p.31

Image 3.11

And even when he shows Lucy in great distress after her miscarriage and her violent encounter with Kyle, Sirk reminds us again, in a beautiful shot, what has kept Lucy faithful so far. (Image 3.11)

This is not at all to say that he is accusing Lucy of thinking of Kyle only in self-interested and greedy ways. All the visual details suggest that Lucy is sincere and in her own mind has convinced herself that she married for love. Sirk is rather showing us that sincerity is not the point, showing us what she doesn't see, can't allow herself to see, and is ironically showing us what isn't in their marriage: the easy intimacy and warmth, not to mention moments of joy, that we expect in a married couple.[7]

There is a ball at the Hadley mansion to introduce Lucy to the high society of the town and Sirk fully indulges his flair for colour and camera movement, ironically reminding us of the crudeness of our moral categories by clothing Marylee in black and Lucy in white. And he

---

[7]Sirk admired Bacall's face as showing 'an almost designing quality', and like her look of coolness; 'she is not a lover'. J. Harvey, 'Sirkumstanial Evidence', p. 55.

makes the banality of the company quite obvious, eavesdropping on the vapid conversations. And Marylee makes the usual spectacle of herself, dancing wildly and sensually, drawing all the attention to herself.

Kyle has suspected something is wrong with his fertility and at the party makes an appointment to see the doctor, who tells him the next day that he does have a problem that will make conceiving difficult but not impossible. Kyle thinks this simply means that he is completely infertile and in a sense he is. He has no productive or procreative power. He can't carry on the business (what kind of life goal would that be anyway? Building more oil wells? What would be the point? The phallic oil derricks we see so often in the film, the source of the Hadley wealth, are ironic images of potency. None of the Hadleys has any power to get what they want; Jasper for his children, Marylee for Mitch, Kyle for Lucy and a family, 'to get off the merry-go-round')[8] and he stands for nothing else in life, has nothing to pass on, seems to want a child only to manifest his virility. But his plight is also linked to the Hadley's in general; he is representative of a world that is itself sterile. And so he tries to return to his early years of cheap bars and rough corn liquor, theatrically playing the role of a rural native. (It is his version of what he thinks his father admires; rough-hewn simple, practical men. It is as if he embodies a version of that ideal in order to say to his father that this, this rowdy, hard-drinking brute, is the only version of the ideal he can manage. He would not be far wrong if he also means to express somehow his sense of the reality of that ideal; not the idealized lone hunter/rancher, but abusive, resentment filled men. We will see a similar dynamic in Marylee later.) In other words,

---

[8]See the discussion in M. Stern, *Douglas Sirk* (Boston: Twain Publishers, 1979), p. 135ff.

Kyle's sense of worthlessness, and his anger about being made to feel this way, his emotional fragility in general, is not just individually pathological. There is something both pathetic and genuine about his sense that there is no deep value to all the money he has (it exists to be spent, wasted; it means nothing), and the same can be said of his desperate need to be loved, to be valued for something other than his money. If taking such pride in social class, money, moral rectitude, celebrity or race are so unsatisfying, then the need to be affirmed in romantic love becomes all the more desperate. Despite our suspicions, he really did love Lucy and needed to be loved by her, and loved as a romantic partner, not in the maternal, care-taker way she assumes.

The fourth chapter of the film, the dissolution of the family and the death of Kyle we have already seen, begins with the death of the patriarch, who dies, one can say, of shame. Marylee had been brought home by the police, after she had picked up a gas station attendant and gone to a motel, humiliating her father more than he can stand. But what is so strange, bizarre even, is that Sirk links Jaspar's death with an erotic solo dance performed by Marylee while she holds a photograph of Mitch, intercut with Jaspar's death. The scene borders on the surreal, and is certainly anti-naturalistic and highly symbolic. Although Marylee is wearing a negligée and dancing suggestively, the dance is not sexually expressive. It is ersatz sex, a testament to how little control she or anyone has over romantic sexuality, and quite sad, frenzied and desperate and alone more than libidinal.[9] It also seems to

---

[9]Se the good discussion about sexuality in the film by Stern, *Sirk*, p.142 ff., and his 'Patterns of Power and Potency, Repression and Violence: An Introduction to the Films of Douglas Sirk', in *The Velvet Light Trap*, Fall 1976, n. 16, pp. 15–21. While catty, Stern's remark about Kyle rings true: he sleeps with a gun under his pillow rather than between his legs.

embody the moral nihilism that the patriarch has created, with the best will in the world, by holding his children to a naïve and self-deceived fantasy of self-reliance and authenticity.[10] That is, this time, Marylee's behaviour, picking up a random gas station attendant and talking him to a motel in her spectacularly noticeable car, has finally gone far enough to wound her father, to make painfully clear to him how badly he has fouled the lives of his children. Marylee, somewhat justifiably, thinks her father tried simply to arrange that Mitch would marry Marylee and settle her down, and by doing so had made that result impossible, had turned Mitch into her brother not her lover. She never expresses her anger, perhaps her hatred of her father, but is given expression in her dance, before she knows that she has gone far enough to prompt his death, and after she had experienced just how wounded he is. For that, she celebrates. At the end of her dance, when Jaspar dies, Sirk photographs Marylee only from the waist down, depersonalizing the dance and suggesting a mere libidinal force, unchecked by already dead conventional mores. And yet again, when photographing Lucy's horror at what happened, he makes sure we see her jewellery, especially the size of her gigantic wedding ring. (Image 3.12)

Jaspar Hadley of course is a sincere, decent man. He does not think of himself as held captive by a naïve fantasy, nor as having damaged his children, and he seems unaware that the entire town is subject to

---

[10]In B. Klinger, 'Much ado about Excess: Genre, Mise-en-Scene and the Woman in *Witten on the Wind*', *Wide Angle* (1989), no. 11.4, she argues that Marylee's expression of a hyperbolic and uncontrollable female sexuality is destructive for her, but also for the family and Jasper, who pays the price for being a conventional (patriarchal) father, in that role unknowingly destroying his children, pp. 8–9.

Image 3.12

his personal whim, that he has the power of a feudal baron, with even the police doing his bidding. But the insignificance of his life, the 'silent damage' he has inflicted on his children, and the fact that the film shows no mourning nor even grief at his passing, is signalled by one brief scene. This moment is so obviously staged to make a point, it is another example of how that staginess can manifest the director's intention; we see the artifice and wonder why it is there. As the servant takes down the mourning wreath, its black ribbon breaks free and tumbles aimlessly (in the wind of course), in effect blowing away as aimlessly as Jaspar's life.[11] (Image 3.13)

Sirk's visual narration is important as the attraction between Lucy and Mitch intensifies, and he finally declares to her how he feels. But

[11]Elsaesser is right that this scene is not part of the normal diegetic flow of the film. It is clearly staged by Sirk to draw attention to something that is not present in the dialogue or action or even facial expressions: what is absent from the film, any intense suffering at the loss of the patriarch and the rapid return to what passes for normality. 'Tales of Sound and Fury', p. 53.

Image 3.13

Sirk stages the revelation in a back alley, a *mise en scène* that stands out in the film as one of the few without opulence, and in muted, drab colours.

The audience will want the 'good people' in the film to triumph over the selfish, thoughtless, 'bad people', so they will likely ignore the setting and its faint suggestion of tawdriness, and this is certainly a scene between two characters who think of themselves as doing the right thing, Mitch by planning to leave and Lucy by rejecting him, but who are signalling to each other otherwise: Lucy by implying that her remaining with Kyle is because of the baby and were it not for that, who knows? (She does not say she loves Kyle or wants to stay; the message is that she is trapped.) And Mitch by suggesting that if she were to give him any encouragement, he would stay. (This scene gets the full melodramatic treatment, especially with the overwrought and far too obvious music.)

The scene that provokes Kyle's striking Lucy and trying to murder Mitch, begins with Marylee's provocation. (She is now dressed in both black and white; almost as if to say that what she will tell Kyle is untrue, but only literally.) Some sort of betrayal of strict fidelity has already occurred between his best friend and his wife. This scene ends with Kyle's rather obvious expression of deep self-loathing, as he throws his whisky at his own image. (The scene has the best line in the film. When Kyle tells Marylee that she is a 'filthy liar', she responds, 'I'm filth, period!')

When she returns from the doctor, Lucy tells Kyle she is pregnant and is dumbfounded by his enraged response. (We see that Lucy's face is not entirely convincing when she denies the charge that the baby is Mitch's. A flicker of guilt about her romantic interest in Mitch crosses her face.) He strikes her, Mitch hears her fall and throws him out of the house, pledging to kill him if he returns, and after heavy drinking Kyle does return. We see a typical melodramatic dénouement, and again Sirk's style is so excessive, it calls attention to itself to such a degree, that it borders on, but never crosses over into, parody. Despite the excess, there is genuine pathos in Kyle's fate. The enmity of Mitch toward Kyle is quite important. Kyle in his naïveté and need, had clearly believed in Mitch's friendship and is stunned (as we should be, but are not) by this revelation that Mitch was never his friend, always resented him deeply, something Mitch makes brutally clear in their dialogue.

In the aftermath, the fifth chapter, Marylee, in her nostalgic 'river outfit', threatens Mitch that she will tell the police he actually murdered Kyle unless Mitch agrees to run away with her and marry her. Mitch is disgusted but we are unsure what Marylee will do at the actual inquest.

There, Marylee, again in rather spectacular black (as, by the way, was Lucy in her last scene with Kyle), at first does implicate Mitch, but

Image 3.14

then in an unexpected, generous turn, exonerates him and tells the truth. In doing so, she utters the truest line in the film, expressing what is very likely the film's point of view as well, although still not the viewer's. She explains, 'My brother always drank too much. He was sad; the saddest of us all. He needed so much. And had so little.'[12] If we were to take seriously this last line, that one of the richest men in the world, 'had so little', then our question about why this should have been so would have sent us back through the film again, questioning our first reading. (Image 3.14)

---

[12]As H. Wegner points out, Sirk's preference for characters like Kyle is clear from his Halliday interviews: 'The type of character I have always been interested in, in the theatre as well as in the movies, and which I also tried to retain in melodrama, is the doubtful, the ambiguous, the uncertainty. Uncertainty and the vagueness of men's aims are central to many of my aims, however hidden these characteristics may be.' *Sirk on Sirk*, p. 47, cited in Wegner, Melodrama as Tragic Rondo – Douglas Sirk's *Written on the Wind*, in *Literature/Film Quarterly* (1982) 10.3, p. 156. It is important to note the last phrase. I think Sirk means to say that the uncertainty of someone about their own aims can be hidden from themselves, not just from others.

Image 3.15

The brief concluding scene of the film is drenched in irony. The wildest and most uncontrollable character in the film, Marylee, is now dressed in a way that suggests her total embourgeoisement, complete with its Freudian suggestion, as Marylee strokes a gold model oil derrick, that the only vital erotic attachment possible in this society is money, and inevitably 'male' money at that. (Image 3.15)

Her deep sadness is not at all meant ironically. She was, after all, the only one in the film who clearly and unconditionally loved someone, and she has now lost him forever. Given the attempt at a kind of epic generality about America in the opening scene, this conclusion is not a pretty picture of the spiritual fate of the company and country. And the happy ending shows us two people driving away in smug self-satisfaction that they deserve the happiness they look forward to, turning their backs on the Hadleys after they had extracted the most value they could out of them. No sadness, no responsibility, no sense of their own guilt for what has happened. (Image 3.16)

Image 3.16

The German director most influenced by Sirk, and he was massively influenced, Rainer Werner Fassbinder, put the Sirkian ethos in an extreme way, but it has the ring of truth.

> ... as a spectator I follow with Douglas Sirk the traces of human despair. In *Written on the Wind* the good, the 'normal', the 'beautiful' are always utterly revolting; the evil, the weak, the dissolute arouse one's compassion.[13]

My claim has been that Sirk has meant to show that the 'good' couple's self-satisfaction in their own virtue is mirrored and ironicized in the willingness of most audiences to identify with these characters, something that reflects their own self-satisfaction. By ironicized, I mean that Sirk has also shown, mostly by visual means, that the characters' self-satisfaction is unwarranted, they are far more disloyal, insensitive and self-interested than they could ever admit to

---

[13]M. Töteberg and L. Lensing, eds. *The Anarchy of the Imagination: Interviews, Essays, Notes. Rainer Werner Fassbinder* (Baltimore: Johns Hopkins University Press, 1992), p. 82.

themselves, although – and this is where things get so interesting – not in any way that would justify an accusation of anything like deliberate manipulation of Kyle for their own ends, or a conscious indifference to or contempt for or cruelty towards Marylee. The same irony is involved in showing the audience their own need for melodrama, and what it can blind them to. But we can now ask: what is the point of such an exercise? It certainly is not to show that an attentive viewer, sensitive to irony, adept at 'decoding' the surface meaning, noticing the duality in the film, is simply cleverer than the average viewer, 'in on the joke', and superior to both the characters and mass audiences. That would be another example of a smug self-certainty that all of Sirk's films work to undermine and would make the art of interpretation a mere game, a search for keys to open the door to the 'other' movie beneath the obvious one. But what then?

The difficulty in understanding the film arises partly from the fact that the language necessary to get into the film inevitably suggests moral distinctions that the film also works, if not to undermine, then to suspend in some way. Kyle Hadley thinks money can buy him anything he wants, and so we seem encouraged to feel morally superior to him. But *he* clearly also knows that this is not true, that his vast wealth actually makes it much harder for him to be genuinely acknowledged and loved, but he is nevertheless trapped by it. And his father has clearly always treated him as a 'failed Mitch' (something most audiences easily accept themselves) not his own person, and this has more than a psychological significance, reflects a long-standing American ambivalence about its own modernization (something also prominent in the claims for a Southern or plantation way of life, a sentiment that played such a role in the antebellum South; this is Texas after all, a slave state) and a reliance on some fantasy about frontier virtue. And his closest friend turns out to have always resented him; had never had the courage to act on that resentment and simply leave. But here too, the Hadleys are in fact Mitch's best chance to escape rural simplicity. Marylee has been psychologically warped by the extreme 'mythologization of Mitch' and those supposed frontier virtues, an attraction that is difficult to disentangle from her own need to please her father. And Kyle's wife, while technically faithful and dutifully caring, married Kyle after one day and night of exposure to his wealth and never gave him what he wanted: open and generous love.

None of this has to do with excusing anyone but none of it has to do with blaming anyone either. The characters are sincere, and their blindness about themselves is treated as almost unavoidable. The entanglement of social and psychological issues in the film makes either response simplistic. It is Jaspar Hadley's vision of what counts as genuine standing in the world (everyone seems to take for granted that while they rely a great deal on money for their status, it is ultimately unsatisfying) that turns out to shadow or 'darken' the chances for genuine love in the film. This is not so much because of that standard itself, but because it is a compensatory and reactive fantasy, unattainable and dangerous. And what is interesting is that Sirk does not treat this as a peculiarity of the individual, Jaspar, or of Texas. As noted, it shows up in his use of Thoreau and the fantasy of self-reliance in *All That Heaven Allows* and the nostalgia he evokes in his invocation of Cather's *My Antonia* in *Tarnished Angels*, he is trying to say something about the character of the American imaginary.

The destructiveness of that imaginary lies behind the cinematic irony of *Written on the Wind*. But the fact that the characters are not as they think of themselves, or that the audience by and large accepts the 'good characters' version of themselves (what the irony reveals) is not a matter of simple hypocrisy or self-serving ambition, or, on the part of the audience, simple gullibility. There is some suggestion of self-deceit in the film, but the paradox of self-deceit requires that one know something about oneself that one, as it is said, hides from oneself. But Mitch and Lucy suffer from a kind of deep blindness about themselves, and not just as a matter of an individual psychological weakness. There is nothing in the world they live in that could disturb their self-certainty, and there are tremendous incentives for them to view the Hadleys as dissolute and themselves as righteous, chief among which is their sense of status as the 'anti-Hadleys', the 'at least virtuous even if not wealthy' bourgeoisie. For all of these reasons, the sincerity of their first-person emotional expressions does not guarantee their genuineness.

The situation is different for the viewers. For one thing, there can be a great difference between a first viewing of a film and a second or third viewing, so there can be a way that the stereotypical melodramatic tropes originally accepted can be undermined by discrepancies, inconsistencies, odd exaggerations, details originally unnoticed. It is of course always possible that the experience of watching a film can remain passive, lazy, even obtuse, or, in the case of melodrama, blinded by assumptions about high and low art. And often characters failing to see what they need to in a story, or audiences' failing to see what is there to see in a melodrama, is the result of an unknowingness that is not culpable, not 'what any reasonable person should have seen', but another reflection of the power of social determinants and what they allow people to see and feel and what they make too hard or too risky to see. And if that is so, it makes the application of moral categories exponentially more difficult, at least without a narrow moralism. But there is also a chance that one can come to see melodramatic excess as much as a comment on such excess than an indulgence of it, or can see that a character's excessive emotionality is not a matter of bad acting or directing, but a sign of some social desperation, some need that is systematically ignored, and the unsatisfactoriness of melodramatic happy endings can look not like a cliché, but as a provocation to understand why it is unsatisfying. Such a range of cinematic experiences will then determine whether the final contrasting images in *Written on the Wind* will seem either like a cruel but deserved fate for Marylee, imprisoned in isolation, comforted erotically only by her wealth and oil well, with Mitch and Lucy liberated from the Hadley influence, off to live happily ever after, or like the crude reality, the truth, of the actual values in this social world, with Mitch and Lucy thoughtlessly wrapped in a comforting but very fragile delusion of happiness.

4

Living Theatre in *Imitation of Life*

Douglas Sirk's last American film, the commercial hit, *Imitation of Life* (1959) is a dual plot movie. What appears to be the main plot concerns the early struggles and eventual success of an aspiring Broadway actress, Lora Meredith (played by Lana Turner). Turner was thirty-eight when the movie was made, and although the character Lora is meant to be somewhat younger, probably early thirties, Lora is clearly not an ingenue. She is told directly that she is 'not a spring chicken,'[1] and that her age will be a serious impediment to her finding work as a beginning actress. (We learn that Lora and her husband, before he died, had worked together in a local professional theatre in their home town and that this is the reason she is starting so late.) The 'ascent to fame and fortune plot' has folded within it Lora's relation to her daughter Susie (played by Terry Burnham as a six-year-old in the first part of the film and by Sandra Dee, in her all-too-recognizable

---

[1] *Imitation of Life* (1959, Universal), directed by Douglas Sirk; screenplay by Eleanor Griffin and Alan Scott. All screengrabs from this film were made by me.

Sandra Dee style, as a sixteen-year-old in the latter half of the film.) At the start of the film, when Lora is poor and just starting out, she happens upon a black woman, Annie Johnson (played brilliantly by Juanita Moore) who also has a young daughter, Sarah Jane (played as an eight-year-old by Karin Decker, and as an eighteen-year-old by Susan Kohner). Annie needs a job; she even needs, when they first meet, a place to live, is homeless, and asks to work as Lora's maid, for no salary, in exchange for a place to live. They thus form an all-female household, without men at the beginning and throughout, but the women never form a bond with each other or, more surprisingly, with their own children.[2] Annie and Sarah Jane accompany Lora and Susie in Lora's rise to the top of Broadway and eventual film stardom.

The second plot is the more intense and is at the heart of the film's wrenching melodrama. Lora is at first confused by the relation between Annie and Sarah Jane, because while Annie is clearly an African American woman, Sarah Jane is very light-skinned, leading Lora at first to believe that Annie is Sarah Jane's nanny. Annie explains that Sarah Jane's father was 'practically white' himself (and that he left shortly after Sarah Jane was born), and that people are always making that mistake. As this plot develops, we learn quickly that Sarah Jane is a very angry child and what she is angry and resentful about is that she is treated as a black person (because of her mother), when she knows she could pass for white. (She is right; she has no trouble passing for white in school and with friends.) This is completely unacceptable to Annie who regards it as a sin to pretend to be what you are not. But Sarah Jane is

---

[2] See M. Selig, 'Contradiction and Reading: Social Class and Sex Class in Imitation of Life', in *Wide Angle*, 1988, 10.4, pp. 13–23.

crystal clear about what 'being who she really is' will mean for her, for her entire life, and she will not compromise, eventually forcing a split with her mother that is as painful as any in any melodrama.

There is an obvious link between the two plots – the concept of imitation announced in the title. In the most obvious sense, Lora wants to make her living by imitating, pretending to be, fictional characters on stage, and it turns out that she is good enough at that to achieve great fame and wealth. Since the middle-class world Sirk depicts in these Universal films is so often characterizable as theatrical (e.g. the maintenance of social class divisions requires constant pretence and rather rigid role playing; and the almost inevitable hypocrisy of self-righteous moral rectitude suggests a similar duality, between a mere pose and a self-interested reality), we wonder immediately if Lora's professional ambition also reflects on her personal 'roles' (staged, or *mere* roles) as mother to Susie, friend to Annie, and lover to Steve (John Gavin's character) at first, in her ascending phase, and then to the producer David Edwards (played by Dan O'Herlihy) when she becomes famous (largely through the patronage of her lover, Edwards). This is an explicit theme in the movie too. Lora is not infrequently told to 'stop acting' (by Steve and especially by her daughter Susie) and there are several scenes where Sirk is clearly making use of Lana Turner's rather limited acting talent to display Lora's stagey, posturing performances. The first time Lora tries to get in to see a theatrical agent, she must pretend to be someone else, a strategy that may not stop when she is 'being herself'.

And there is the linked imitation theme, Sarah Jane's attempt to 'imitate', to pass as, perform as, white. Interestingly, the career she chooses as the vehicle of the imitation is show business, as if to suggest that if she can get an audience to regard her as white, 'perform' so well as a white dancer in cabaret shows, she will have succeeded in being white. (She often simply insists, 'I *am* white.') The show business career she has available to her, though, is that of an exotic dancer (as close as the times would allow to being a stripper), and then a chorus girl. This tawdriness seems a comment on Lora's very limited, and so somewhat tawdry, conception of her acting career, interested from the beginning only in success and fame.[3] It is a telling remark early on when she is told there are no parts for her in Tennessee Williams's play; light comedy is more her style.

And all of this already connects with Sirkian themes we have been noting. What it means to have achieved some standing as who you take yourself and your virtues to be is obviously a social phenomenon. Such standing is acknowledgement by relevant others. By contrast, it is a source of great anxiety and self-doubt if, however significant and worthy one regards oneself, one is nevertheless either invisible in that social world, or is systemically misrecognized, if one is regularly regarded as other than one is. (Cary and Ron have this problem in *All That Heaven Allows*; Kyle and Marylee in *Written on the Wind*.) But such standing is not a *wholly* matter-of-fact social phenomenon. If one has achieved a certain measure of respect as 'who one has merely been pretending to be', if the standing has been achieved by strategic or manipulative means, then such standing and respect have no value, cannot be a source of pride. If Lora's self-image is what she assumes a 'great actress' and especially a 'mother' should be, must be to be

---

[3] On the similarities and contrast between the banality of Lora's career success and the depravation and failure of Sarah Jane's, see Selig, 'Contradiction', pp.17ff.

acknowledged as such, and she seeks to perform such roles, always with an eye to the audience, then the results cannot be satisfying. Or, they should not be. Complicating matters is the power of self-blindness and self-deceit. As we shall see, even when her illusions about being Annie's friend are shattered, not much seems to sink in; Lora is hardly devastated. And not simply because she is selfish and thoughtless. The film manages to show us socially powerful reasons for such traits. That is, all of this is all true even though Lora's case is not one of outright scheming, hypocrisy and manipulation. As we saw with the other Sirk films, subjective sincerity is no guarantee of genuineness. Likewise, Sarah Jane will never become white, no matter if the whole world takes her to be so, and this for a heart-breaking reason in the film. The only way she can even partially succeed is by disowning, in effect, her mother, keeping her hidden away from her friends, establishing as much distance between them as she can. (Anytime Annie shows up in Sarah Jane's life, her passing is exposed and she is humiliated.) She has to live with that rejection throughout the last part of the film, and we see that it is all more painful than she can admit to herself.[4]

One other element ties the two plots together. A far too harsh way of putting it would be that the two mothers, having had to make their

---

[4]Lora's ambition to achieve a certain kind of cultural status (as opposed to any interest in being a great artist) is connected to its historical moment too, what sociologists of the time called 'status panic' for the new middle class. An indispensable discussion of the issue: M. Conroy, '"No sin in lookin' prosperous": Gender, Race and the Class Formations of Middlebrow Taste in Douglas Sirk's *Imitation of Life*', in *The Hidden Foundation: Cinema and the Question of Class*, ed. D. James, R. Berg (Minneapolis: University of Minnesota Press, 1996), pp. 114–37. As Conroy points out, the cultural status Lora wants is an imitation of culture, not the thing itself. For more on the historical decade represented in the film, see L. Fischer, 'Three-Way Mirror: *Imitation of Life*', in *Imitation of Life: Douglas Sirk, Director*, ed. L. Fischer (New Brunswick: Rutgers University Press, 1991), pp. 3–28.

way in the world alone, however full of good will for their daughters, are 'failed' mothers, fail their daughters in ways that are painfully pointed out to them by the daughters. Perhaps it would be better to say that both daughters accuse their mothers of having failed them, but we have some sympathy with the charge, even if not completely with the idea of individual blame. We will have to deal with that charge and the meaning of a Sirkian supposed happy-ending-reconciliation scene one more time. It is too harsh because they are obviously also loving mothers, and the psychological dynamics of their relation to their daughters are not at all isolated by Sirk as simply the failures of individuals. (It would also be too harsh by being far too simplistic and it would associate such a reading with a not at all uncommon reaction to the film, that it was a critique of 'working mothers' in the postwar era, that women at work were 'acting' in theatrical roles they should not be playing, imitating the life of men, given their 'natural' place in the home raising children while husbands work.) Such a critique not only misses the obvious fact that these women are not working out of frivolous vanity. The domain of work is the domain of necessity; they have no choice. And it ignores Sirk's irony in having the most censorious character on this theme, Steve, come off as a patronizing bore, somehow having convinced himself that advertising for a beer company is much more important than anything Lora could possibly do. The extraordinary American celebration of celebrity and fame, and so the creation of the widespread, burning need to be seen, to have some small measure of such renown, that sort of standing, even if for five minutes on Facebook or YouTube or Twitter nowadays, is not an invention of Lora. She is as much its victim as its agent. And the soul-destroying consequences of racism, so extensive and so deep that even the very experienced and wise Annie cannot imagine how damaging it looks to her daughter, is simply what Annie has had to face all her life, not what she can in any way control. That is, she can't control how she is seen, and that is the great temptation (and fantasy) for Sarah Jane, that she can.

In the case of Lora and Susie, the putative failure is a simple matter of neglect, a matter of Lora's career always coming first. (Whereas in *Stella Dallas*, when Stella appreciates the irreconcilable tension between her own class ambitions and motherhood, she thinks she must sacrifice herself, efface herself and those ambitions, to be a good mother; in this film, Lora barely notices the conflict [which is nonetheless quite real] and sacrifices her daughter. At least that is the way Susie sees it and she has cause.) Susie is basically raised by Annie and both Annie and Susie know this; the realization comes to Lora quite late in the film. In the case of Annie and Sarah Jane, it is again nothing simply culpable, but nevertheless, as Annie realizes, she hadn't imagined, hadn't let herself imagine, what the world must look like to Sarah Jane, why Annie's world of segregated church, church socials, 'making do', 'being patient', repressing anger and trying just to get along, would look so false and so hopeless to Sarah Jane, given what might be possible for her. This is all especially so for Sarah Jane (and not seen, perhaps a bit wilfully not seen, by Annie) because while Sarah Jane has been raised as, theoretically, Susie's friend and equal, Sarah Jane must everyday experience the difference between the private school Susie gets to go to and the public school she must attend, not to mention Susie's riding lessons, expensive camps and trips and clothes, etc. Sarah and Annie are even assigned their own back entrance in the new suburban mansion Lora moves them all into, and back stairs to their bedrooms, and it does not seem to have occurred to Annie how invisible this must all make Sarah Jane feel; how angry.

But this is only a rough sketch of the dual plot structure, the theme of imitation, and the place of the film in Sirk's oeuvre. Things will get more complicated quickly in a close consideration of the film's details.

The film opens with quite an unusual credit sequence. We see a black background and begin to hear a Sammy Fain/Paul Francis Webster ballad, 'Imitation of Life', which tells us that a life without love is not really life, but a mere imitation of life. (Actually, just as with *Written on the Wind*, we hear first thunderous, ominous chords, creating an atmosphere of foreboding, before a musically smooth transition into a melodious, romantic variation on that theme, a signal of the duality of the melodrama.) The idea expressed goes very far: the essence of life itself is to love and be loved; without that, we are not living but imitating life. But why 'imitating'? why not: absent love, we have a less satisfying life, we have missed something? The idea seems to be that genuine love is impossible if one lives a theatrical, posing, self-seeking life. Love, and therewith life, requires genuineness, exposure to risk, willing to accept such risk, giving up the illusion of control, selflessness, allowing oneself to be caught up in life, at its most intense in love, rather than plotting out a life for one's own advantage. That would be imitating what life genuinely is: such exposure, chance and risk. If we remember that sentiment after we have seen the film, we will note uneasily that there is only one example of uncompromisingly selfless love in the film, Annie's for Sarah Jane, and we know that that has not prevented several imitations. Annie's life with Lora is not at all hypocritical but it reveals, expresses, nothing of her true life, which, Annie realizes, Lora knows nothing about because she cares nothing about it. As we shall see, we the viewers have also only seen the Annie she needs to be to have her role in Lora's household, an imitation Annie, not the 'real' one, performing the role she needs to. It will be as much of a surprise to the viewers as to Lora when we learn at the end of the film about the scores of friends and 'non-Lora' experiences that make up the true Annie. And her mother love does not prevent or dissuade Sarah Jane from her own life of imitation. The romantic relations, Lora's with first Steve and then David, do not amount to much. Whatever love she has for Steve is not strong enough to prompt any compromise with her career,[5] and her love affair with David seems straightforwardly strategic and passionless. (After she becomes successful she tells Annie that David wants to marry her. Annie asks if she loves him and she answers honestly, 'No. But he's good for me. At least I try to tell myself he's good for me.') As we have already suggested, Lora's love for Susie could not be called selfless.

In a nice Sirkian touch, one could be mistaken for thinking that the ballad we hear is being sung by one the most popular vocalists of the time, Nat King Cole, but we learn at the end of the credits that it is in effect a nearly perfect imitation of that singer's sound and style, sung by Earl Grant. Stranger still, we begin to see small shiny objects float down and fall in front of us as we read the credits. They look like tiny

---

[5]Although she shouldn't. Sirk goes out of his way to characterize Steve as well-meaning but clueless and patronizing. When he re-appears in the film's second half, in case we have forgotten what a stuffed shirt he is, Sirk poses him with a pipe and an even more pretentious air.

Image 4.1

transparent stones, and we eventually see them as costume jewellery, imitations, that begin to build up a wall in front of us, finally filling the whole screen, as if to block us from seeing what is behind it. This could be a suggestion that the viewers will see, will want to see, only the surface melodrama, an imitation of the 'real movie', something that will block out Sirk's irony and so that 'other film', a film quite a bit more critical and subversive. (Image 4.1)

The narration begins with three different angled shots of the same extremely crowded Coney Island beach, as if to repeat and emphasize the anonymity or 'lost in a crowd' feel in much modern society. And someone *is* lost, Susie. It is telling that the first we see of Lora, she has lost her daughter, and it is of course equally telling that it is Annie who has found her and is taking care of her until she is found. (Although homeless, she has spent her own money on food for the children, hot dogs.) It does not occur to Lora to offer to pay her share. (Image 4.2)

Image 4.2

We see the frantic Lora (she is in sunglasses; no one else we see in any of the opening sunny beach scene is in sunglasses, making a small point about Lora's obscured vision) leaning over a sign that informs us that it is 1947 (we are about to pass through ten years of Lora's ascent to fame and fortune) but the sign is itself puzzling. It announces that the 1947 Mardi Gras is coming, but it tells us that that will occur on September 8–14. Mardi Gras of course occurs forty days before Easter and occurs in February, and if Coney Island will celebrate Mardi Gras in September, it would have to be an 'imitation' Mardi Gras. Lora is photographed by Steve, the first indication of what will amount to her claim to status or standing, 'to be seen' and is helped by him to find a policeman and eventually Susie.

Lora finally agrees to Annie's offer, but before the Broadway star plot begins, we see a couple of disturbing scenes of the children. When they play on the beach, they make fun rather cruelly of a fat man who is asleep, setting a beer can on his stomach and laughing at it going up and down. This is not all that unusual for children of that age, but again they are playing unsupervised; neither mother has an eye out for the children on a crowded beach. Steve takes a picture and, when the man awakens, embarrassed and angry, Steve 'imitates', pretends he is, the father neither girl has, and he promises he will punish them. He does not of course, and is hostile to Lora, explaining to the man that Lora not only spoils her daughter, 'she goes around losing her'. (He means, again.) When they return to the apartment, Susie offers Sarah Jane one of her dolls as a gift, a black doll. Sarah Jane rejects the gift and takes Susie's doll away from her. Annie makes her return it, but Sarah Jane complains that they always have to live 'in the back' and contemptuously drops the black doll. Annie later explains to Lora, 'We just came from a place where our colour deviled my baby,' but we hear no further explanation; we simply know that Sarah Jane's anger at being taken as black has cause. It is not spontaneous and unmotivated.

Annie quickly assumes the roles of wife to Lora and mother to Susie, gets the household organized, sorts out their finances, takes on extra work in the building, and Lora is freed up to make the rounds of theatrical agents. She pretends to be the client of a big Hollywood producer and gets in to see an agent, Allen Loomis (played by Robert Alda). But he eventually turns out to be a lecherous 'casting couch' type and she has to walk out on him. There is some ambiguity in the film about her understanding of what is expected of her before this happens. If it is so clear cut to the viewer what type Loomis is and what he wants (Steve certainly understands or fears the worst) how can it not be clear to Lora? She somehow convinces herself (no doubt like so many before her) that she can handle it. She can't and is deeply disappointed.

But the connection with Loomis does issue in a small job, a dog powder commercial that is played for comic effect. But it occasions a classic lucky break. One of Loomis's friends, a powerful playwright, David Edwards (played by Dan O'Herlihy), had seen the ad and thought Lora would be perfect for a small role in his next play. She auditions and courageously resists some of the direction and writing, and instead of being fired, she is promoted to a much more important role, is a critical success, and her big time career is launched.

But there is trouble at home. On a rainy day, Annie realizes that Sarah Jane doesn't have her bright red rain boots and goes to her school to give them to her. When she arrives, she realizes that the teacher and the school have no idea that Sarah Jane is black; that is, Annie realizes that her daughter has been passing for white. Interestingly, this, pretending to be white, is how Annie sees it but that denies at least some of the ambiguity of the situation. Sarah Jane has a point when she says that no one asked her her race, and if they don't ask, why should she make a point of telling them? If everyone thinks she is white, does that not make her in some sense of the word at least, white? And if not, exactly why not? Annie of course realizes that once you know that people assume you are white, and you don't correct them, it is only a matter of time before you have to lie actively and take steps to deceive others about your relatives, and all that apart from the effect on you if you know you are living a false life. But Sarah Jane, in terms of the largest theme in the film, is asking something like the question that emerges in art forgery. If no one, no expert in the world, can tell the difference between a genuine and a fake painting, if the aesthetic qualities are indistinguishable, what besides a merely contingent date qualifies one as priceless and the other as criminal.

Image 4.3

And Sarah Jane would not admit to any damaging effects for her performance; just the opposite as far as she is concerned.[6] This is an issue we will have to return to at the end of the film. Annie seems to come to a different view of all this, but the issue becomes quite complicated.

Sarah Jane bolts from the classroom into the rain, furious with her mother, telling her she hopes she, Annie, will die, and that she doesn't understand why Annie has to be her mother (and so why she has to be black). (Image 4.3)

Annie is devastated and returns home as discouraged, sad and beaten down as we ever see her in the film. It is among the most painful scenes to watch in all of melodrama. Annie is far and away the

---

[6]It is almost as if Sarah Jane is anticipating the 'anti-essentialist' idea that race and gender are performances, social roles. If that is true, though, the performances have to succeed, and all succeed can mean is being taken for real by a social audience. But if that is all there is to being a woman or being black, then there are no constraints on what success counts as, and in that case there is nothing left of the notion of success, performance, roles, etc.

Image 4.4

most insightful and the kindest character in the film and to see her so terribly wounded by her own child, and not for anything she has done, but simply for her fate, to see her the object of such anger and what seems even hatred from her own daughter is hard to take. When she is back in the apartment, Lora, as usual, offers her the banal consolation. 'Don't worry, Annie, I'm sure you will be able to explain things to her.' To which Annie responds, 'How do you explain to your child that she was born to be hurt?'[7] (Image 4.4)

We then see a swift summary of Lora's rise to the top of Broadway, one hit Edwards comedy after another. Throughout the summary of her successful decade, we see that Annie is carried along too, attending to (that is, mothering) the two children, and attending to Lora too.

---

[7]The movie leaves ambiguous what Sarah Jane's status would be in public schools if she had declared herself black. Later in the movie, Sarah Jane's high school appears to be rife with open racism, although whether the racism is still de jure or de facto is not clear, nor much relevant. One can safely infer that she could not go to that school as a black person, and so what Annie is demanding of her would come at quite a cost.

But in the latter case we should begin to note that Annie is largely invisible to Lora except as an extension of herself. Whenever we see her talking with Annie it is almost always about herself and her career and her concerns; we never hear her once asking about Annie's life outside her orbit. I say we should notice, but that is asking a lot on first viewing. We have seen the shabby conditions of the first apartment, how difficult it has been to get established, and we admire Lora's generosity in taking in Annie and Sarah Jane when she did not have much more than they did. We root for her, and if there are moments when she seems vain, or insensitive, if she seems to feel no real pain in giving up Steve, if she leaps into David's very useful arms a bit too quickly, we think that on balance we understand and we try not to be judgemental. But as with the other Sirk melodramas we have discussed, we are, as viewers, to some extent being set up for what happens later ('set up' in the sense that the film will ask us to confront our own blindness). As in so many cases, the fact that Lora is not at all a cynical or manipulative careerist but well-meaning, sincere, confident that she is a generous, good person, are all only partial aspects of the issue raised by her character. When she is called to accounts in the film's last moments first by Susie, then by Steve, and finally by Annie, shown her neglect, self-servingness and blindness, we have to wonder about the normative status of that kind of blindness, how we want to account for and assess such a characteristic. We sometimes hear that there is a form of 'wilful blindness', and we mean a situation in which a person does not merely not 'see' something, like the implications of what she is doing, but succeeds in 'looking away' from what is 'there' to be seen if she would only look, and 'there' in a way that we can tell the agent suspects is there. What complicates matters even more is that, as in so many other cases in Sirk that we have seen, he does not present the blindness, even if wilful in this sense, as in an individual failure of character. That is, Lora is indeed blind to, ignorant of, the effect of her ambition on Steve, Susie, Sarah Jane and Annie. She is indeed a thoughtless, if also well-meaning person. (One measure of her blindness is something Fassbinder points out[8]: she is so often surprised, surprised when Steve abandons his plans for art photography and takes a steady job so they can get married, surprised that Sarah Jane is unhappy, surprised when her daughter berates her for constantly leaving her alone, surprised that Annie has hundreds of friends, even surprised that Annie could do something to her like up and die.) But all of that does not make the effects of her character and the actions it leads to any less emotionally damaging to those around her. Aristotle held that people are responsible for the formation of their character, and it would not be unreasonable to say that Lora should have seen what was there to see, that she is responsible for not seeing it. But again, as in other Sirk films, this would ignore how important having some standing is in modern societies, how important various kinds of public regard, celebrity, fame, are admired and envied for this reason, how formative modern societies are, and how difficult it is to isolate an individual in such a society and hold them personally accountable.

This raises the philosophical problem of the status of 'well-meaning wrong', let us say; cases where another is wronged, and in a way that can be tied to the self-interest of the one wronging the victim, but

---

[8]Fassbinder, R. *The Anarchy of the Imagination: Interviews, Essays, Notes* (Baltimore: Johns Hopkins University Press, 1992), p. 88.

without the usual awareness and indifference we associate with wrong-doing. So many who do so many damaging things to other people always seem to have 'their reasons' and think of themselves as in the right. This is all often bad faith, of course, but bad faith as self-deceit raises a similar issue. If someone has *successfully*, as we say, hidden something they know from themselves (something that paradoxically requires that they also not know they have done the hiding) then, given that success (it *is* hidden from them) what is the right moral assessment? We see that Lora has clearly succeeded and I am suggesting that the film should make us doubt whether the category of individual moral assessment is relevant.

One mark of how difficult this all is is Annie. In a dressing room scene after another success, when Lora tells Annie she doesn't love David, and then mentions she 'hasn't been up to see my baby at school for weeks', she also lets us know, when she is, not at all seriously, entertaining the idea of retiring, that she would then have more time for Susie, she also notes that Annie could then be home much more with Sarah Jane. So Lora's neglect has made necessary a certain sort of neglect by Annie, the paragon of virtue in the film, something we never hear her complain about. (And if Annie is so often in New York as Lora's dresser and factotum, what exactly *is* Sarah Jane's situation?) Moreover when Annie addresses Lora's worry about spending so little time with her daughter, she does not encourage Lora to see how happy it would make Susie if that were true, and instead she says something we will learn is untrue, that we think Annie must know is untrue, that Susie is fine with it all, that she knows Lora loves her, and that Lora 'needs show business as much as show business needs her'. Toeing the party line like this is a mark of a certain sort of complicity with Lora's ambition. If that seems too harsh – that Annie suffers from some level of blindness that is also damaging to the children – we will need to see the two girls' 'explosions' at the end of the film to come to terms with that issue. And it is also true that as time goes on, Annie does try finally to tell Lora that Susie has written her, Annie (does she even write to her mother?), that all the money Lora is spending on Susie is not what Susie wants, that she misses her mother and feels neglected. And in this case, there is a classic case of looking away from what you could have seen, or of wilful blindness. As Annie tries to tell Lora, Lora breaks off, refuses to let Annie finish and asks Annie about her health.

Success means a new house in the New York suburbs. (Image 4.5) After the first half of the film's emphasis on crowded urban life and the cramped apartment (and so on both the difficulty of standing out in any way, as well as the unavoidable intimacy and cooperation required by that situation), the emphasis in the new house is now on the distance between characters, and a kind of cold display, of wealth but also of Lora's new status. When Annie worries about whether they can afford it all, Lora says they 'can't afford not to' have the house. It is a necessary prop in her acting career. And this new situation and her new status will also means a final break with David. Lora, putting on the airs of a true 'artist', explains that she doesn't want to do another comedy, David's latest play, that she is going to do the 'Stewart play' instead, a bit of social realism it turns out.

This scene is the beginning of the reckoning in the film with all that Lora has not seen, with the lack of genuineness in a life that imitates comity, concern and empathy, but that actually has very little of that. The crack in the façade occurs when David objects, telling Laura that

Image 4.5

the role she will play is 'drama, no clothes, no sex'. And he goes on to
say about the play, 'and that coloured angle enters into it; it's absolutely
controversial'. At this point Sirk cuts to a shot of Annie, fixing David's
drink and there is a look of concern and fear on her face. (Image 4.6)
She seems to be afraid that the topic she has spent years helping Lora
avoid, what she and her daughter have had to endure as black people,
will come out in the open in ways she can't manage. Or perhaps she
is afraid that it will come out and Lora's ignorance will be on full
display. Perhaps she will claim a deep knowledge of the 'coloured
problem' from having lived with Annie and Sarah Jane. But Annie
needn't worry. Lora could be said to understand some aspect of the
problem from having seen what Sarah Jane has had to go through, but
she does not, and the blindness here is telling.

As if Lora's blindness were not clear enough, David goes on, 'And
what do you know about controversy?' remarkably, Lora responds,
'nothing, and I don't want to. I only know it's a good script.' That sums
up Lora, and given that shot of Annie, the viewer is left wondering

Image 4.6

what Annie is thinking as she overhears them, discussing the coloured angle with Annie right there in the room.

The last section of the film focuses our attention on the plight of the two daughters. Sandra Dee's Susie is a naïve, sweet child, somewhat cloying, who discusses her problems and her new interest in boys with Annie and whose resentment about her mother's neglect slowly begins to surface. No sooner had Lora promised Susie that she would cut back on her work to spend more time with her (and no sooner had she promised something like that to Steve, who is briefly back in the picture), she reneges on her promise and is thrilled to be considered for a role in a film by the great 'Americo Felluci'. Susie's reaction is quite complicated and a bit creepy in the film. She is of course not quite aware of all the dimensions of her anger at her mother, and she certainly does not consciously plot to 'steal Steve away from her' but the sixteen-year-old convinces herself that she is in love with Steve and has a chance at being a couple with him. The blindness theme is relevant again because it is hard to believe that Steve, who had simply been asked to look after Susie while Lora is away working on the film, as he takes Susie to adult restaurants and goes riding with her together, is not aware of this infatuation, and especially hard to believe that he does nothing to deal with it and gently explain things to Susie. Steve remains as clueless as he has been throughout. But her fantasy about Steve at least has the subconscious goal of finally getting her mother's attention and she is able to tell her mother how neglected and unloved she has felt, and that she will be attending college in Colorado, not nearby.

But the melodramatic punch in the concluding scenes comes from what happens to Sarah Jane, who also finds a way to try to make both Annie and Lora see what they have not seen. When Annie tries to draw Sarah Jane into her segregated world of church and church socials, and even mentions the hope that Sarah Jane might be interested in a young man from that world, Sarah Jane responds angrily, 'busboys, cooks, chauffeurs!' And she evinces open hostility toward Lora, making clear that she realizes that Lora has no clue about or interest in her and her mother's real lives.

That real life is a secret life. It becomes clear that Sarah Jane has been passing for white in her high school and, she admits to Susie, she even has a secret white boyfriend (as white a boyfriend as one could imagine, played by Troy Donahue) and she imagines a future together with him.

Since the move into the new home, it becomes increasingly obvious that Annie is ill and is weakening. As a party is laid on for the director's representative, Sarah Jane is asked to help out and she decides to theatricalize, act out, what she suspects are the stereotypical prejudices of the white guests. She serves appetizers as a kind of cartoon version

Image 4.7

of a black domestic, affecting an exaggerated accent, and balancing the tray on her head. She tells Lora that she learned serving that way from her 'Mammy' who learned it from her 'Massah, before she belonged to you.' (Image 4.7)

She explains to Lora 'my mother was so anxious for me to be coloured, I was going to show you I could be'. She means of course, I was going to show you what I know white people think of coloured people when they think of them at all, show you what it would mean for me to 'become' the black woman I am in the white world I live in now as white, show you that you all have no understanding of how painful it would be for me to do as you say and be the person I am, rather than imitating a white woman. Lora bats away the racial issue and asks how Sarah Jane could have hurt her mother like that. Sarah Jane tries to explain to Lora that she has no idea what it means to be 'different' and Lora defends herself by asking whether she has ever treated Sarah Jane as different. Sarah Jane accepts that Lora has never been intentionally cruel and never explicitly racist to her, but the

Image 4.8

question is preposterous. Sarah Jane has been treated different than
Susie her whole life, and the fact that Lora has never explicitly
demeaned either Annie or Sarah Jane does not mean that she has seen
who they are or has had any interest in who they are. She has been
dealing with simulacra of both of them, the imitations that allow her
to pursue her career and be convinced of her individual virtue. Sirk
photographs the scene so that the irony of Lora's defence of herself is
plainly visible. We see Lora lecturing Sarah Jane about how virtuous
Lora has been, how equal they all are, while clothed in thousands of
dollars of jewellery and made up as the glamorous movie star she now
considers herself to be.[9] (Image 4.8)

---

[9]Sirk was quite explicit about what he wanted from Lana Turner's costumes. In the interview
with Harvey, he is asked: 'Turner's costumes are very garish ; they often seem to be a joke.
Was that intentional?' And Sirk responds, ' Yes, of course.' 'Did she care? Or didn't she
notice?' 'She was very compliant through the whole shooting. She trusted us. And I might
add that she wasn't sorry – she was very happy with the picture.' Harvey, 'Sirkumstantial',
p. 55.

This all is followed by a scene between a somewhat penitent Sarah Jane and a very tired Annie. It is a scene of extraordinary subtlety and power. Sarah Jane has just gone to extreme lengths to show Lora and Annie how difficult it would be simply to accept the advice to 'be who she is' and live in the black, segregated world of Annie when she has a chance to escape it. She is genuinely pained to realize that she has caused Annie so much distress, and she begs her mother, 'please try to understand. I didn't mean to hurt you. I love you.' And she embraces Annie. Annie says, 'Oh, I know baby.' And then, remarkably, given how sympathetic the portrait of Annie has been, she utterly fails to understand anything at all of what Sarah Jane has been trying to tell her. 'You're just like a puppy that's been cooped up too much. That's why I wanted you to go to the party.' (She means the segregated party that Sarah Jane wanted no part of.) Again, Sarah Jane tries to explain how profound the problem is. 'Oh, Mama, don't you see? That won't help.' (Image 4.9)

Several things are going on at once in this exchange. In the simplest sense, Annie really does not 'see' or understand Sarah Jane's situation. The whole crisis had been precipitated by Sarah Jane's furious reaction to Annie's suggestion that she attend a party with 'busboys, cooks, chauffeurs'. And yet Annie returns to the very same suggestion, pretending to herself, I think we have to say, that the problem, despite everything she has just heard, is that Sarah Jane has not 'gotten out' enough. Annie 'should have seen' that the problem is much greater and very different, it would be easy to say, but at the next level of complexity, it is also clear that Annie cannot allow herself to see that problem as it is. She would then see that, although Sarah Jane has lived her whole life in Lora's white world, and lately in Lora's wealthy,

Image 4.9

privileged white world, what Annie is encouraging is that Sarah
Jane should just accept a second-class, diminished status and the
humiliations of racism. Annie does counsel 'patience', and she is
probably referring to the civil rights struggle and its possible success,
but that still assumes that Sarah Jane identify with and socialize with
black people, and announce herself as black in the white world, and
the latter would be a huge price, from Sarah Jane's point of view (given
how she has lived most of her life), for her to pay, for however many
years it takes for such 'patience' to pay off. So Annie too is living in a
state of illusion about her daughter, is blind to what the issue of race
has come to mean to Sarah Jane, and perhaps can be said even to be
'turning away' from what she knows is there to see. But this situation
borders on the tragic, not the melodramatic. Neither one of them can
fix racism, and there is no acceptable way to resign oneself to it and
live with it. The blindness, the strategic blindness we have seen so
often in Sirk, is the only subjective way to live with such a hopeless,
objective situation. This is true of Sarah Jane as well. It is heartless and

cruel of her (not that she sees that) to scorn the 'busboys, cooks and chauffeurs' to her mother, a *domestic*, 'in service' to Lora. Whenever Sarah Jane goes on a rant about being black, it would be hard for her to realize that she is also contemptuously rejecting her mother and her mother's world, accusing her mother of accepting something she should not, although it is clear that Sarah Jane cannot allow herself to understand it in these terms.

As in other cases we have seen I think it is fair to say that Lora wrongs Sarah Jane and Annie by her blindness, not just that she unintentionally harms them, and even that Annie wrongs Sarah Jane by not understanding what she could understand, and Sarah Jane wrongs Annie by her own blindness, but these are all cases of wrong without, however paradoxical it is, there being any wrongdoers. These are not, or not just, individual failings which should be imputable solely to individuals in their weakness.

There are two more implications of the scene. Annie has insisted that Sarah Jane not pretend to be something else, but to be who she is, be genuine. No one, of course, in the segregated world Annie lives in should be assumed to be living a hypocritical or phony life just by living in the segregated world in the way that requires. But it is in a different way a false life, an imitated life, not the life they would lead were they not forced, often violently forced, to live a segregated life. (In terms of the opening song's principle, that without love there is only an imitation of life, one could say that the absence of love, caritas, for everyone in the white world is what requires the dissimulation of segregated life.) It is not 'their' life, a genuine life. They have been prohibited from having such a life. There is of course much that *is* 'theirs', and much resistance, but the basic fact of segregated life

Image 4.10

remains. We realize, as we see Annie fail to understand Sarah Jane, that for the latter, the real import of Annie's imperative is not 'be who you are' or just 'don't hide the fact that you are black', because the implication of the latter has to be, 'Live in the segregated world *white* people have created for us. Live the way white people insist we live.' This would all be extremely difficult for either of them to see.

That there is no way out for either of them, especially for Sarah Jane, no way for her to pass as white without a far more drastic abandonment of her past than she has thus far been willing to do, is brought home to the viewer in a particularly brutal way. She goes to meet her secret white boyfriend Frankie (Troy Donahue), but he has learned that she has a black mother. In the scene, we see Sarah Jane reflected in a bar's window; that is, see her reflection, the imitation she wants to be. (Image 4.10)

Frankie asks' Is it true? Is your mother a nigger?' and he beats Sarah Jane terribly, throwing her into a pool of black oil, leaving her covered in it. (Image 4.11)

Image 4.11

When the beating is discovered, Annie again insists that such lies, passing, will always be found out, and Sarah Jane, beginning her decisive break with her mother, tells her that it wouldn't be discovered if she were not always around.[10]

Second, we see even more clearly something mentioned before, that Annie's 'life-with-Lora' has not been her life, the life she would freely lead, but the life she must lead in Lora's world. There is a conversation between Annie and Lora in which Annie reveals that she has been saving up her whole life for a very grand and expensive funeral. Annie says she has it all written down, exactly how she wants it and the friends she wants to be there. We are set up then for two of the most revealing lines in the film. In the first, Lora says, revealing the true depths of her staggering thoughtlessness, 'It never occurred to

---

[10]It is important to note that Sarah Jane never rejects her mother, never says something like, 'Oh that coloured lady who calls herself my mother? My parents died when I was young and she was my nanny and took care of me but she is not my real mother.' She is still trying to live out, apparently, her childhood strategy: 'Hope they don't ask and never tell.'

me that you had any friends; you never have any visitors.' Annie patiently explains that she knows lots of people, 'hundreds' through her Baptist church and several lodges. Lora says, 'I didn't know,' and Annie, in the second crucial line, tells her, kindly but devastatingly, 'Miss Lora, you never asked.' It is true that Lora has never asked, but it is also true that Annie never felt they were on any real terms of equality such that a free and personal conversation about her personal life, her real life, would have been possible. In a few seconds the imitative quality of her ten years with Lora is revealed.

Sarah Jane first gets work as an exotic dancer in a local club, telling her mother that she is working in a library. Annie discovers the lie and tracks Sarah Jane down to the club and of course, again, Sarah Jane is rejected when they discover she is black. She then moves as far away as she can, to the West Coast and dances in the chorus line in a club. Annie tracks her down again and flies out there, but this time she is going simply to say good-bye. It has become clear to her and to us that she is dying.

This time, for the first time, Annie joins rather than rejects the imitation game Sarah Jane is playing. When she enters Sarah Jane's apartment, she tells her not to worry that 'nobody saw me' (a line dripping with irony; it could describe her whole life in the white world). Annie asks her if she is happy, if she has found what she really wants, and Sarah Jane explains that she has become someone else. 'I am white,' she says (and then ever more pathetically and painfully, 'white … WHITE!') as Sirk photographs them both reflected in a mirror, photographs, that is, the images *both* have projected of themselves in the white world, as if to say that these reflections are who they are, in complete self-alienation. (Image 4.12) Sara Jane is insisting

Image 4.12

that she is white as she looks directly at the pair of them, her mother and her in the same frame, denying what she sees in front of her.[11]

After a heart-breaking embrace, one of Sarah Jane's friends arrives, and assumes Annie is the maid. Annie corrects her and in a remarkable concession to her daughter, in testimony to how much she has indeed finally understood her daughter, she lies, tells the friend that she 'used to take care of' 'Miss Linda' using Sarah Jane's fake name, and leads the friend to believe she was Sarah Jane's nanny. Sarah Jane clearly realizes how much this has cost Annie, what a profound act of love it is, and when she says good-bye, mouths (but still cannot say) the word, 'mama'.[12]

---

[11]Cf. the discussion in Thomas Schatz, 'Douglas Sirk and the Family Melodrama: Hollywood Baroque', *Hollywood Genres: Formulas, Filmmaking, and the Studio System* (New York, 1981), p. 253.

[12]What Annie has finally realized marks the contrast with what she had never realized. Fassbinder typically overstates the matter but there is a great deal of truth in what he says. In noting our tendency to see Sarah Jane as the cruel one and Annie as the pitiable object of the cruelty, he remarks, 'But, in fact, it's exactly the opposite. The mother who wants to possess her child because she loves her is brutal. And Sarah Jane is defending herself against her mother's terrorism, against the world's terrorism.' *The Anarchy of the Imagination*, p. 89.

In Annie's death scene, she pleads with Lora to find Sarah Jane and tell her that she is sorry for 'being selfish', for loving her too much, to explain that it was because it was 'all she had' (something that can seem like a parental cliché but is quite painfully true in this case). And in a last reference to the film's theme, she asks the minister present to give his wife her fur scarf, noting that she was sure the wife never believed it was 'genuine mink'. The minister insists that his wife did believe her, and we have our last note about the difficulty of living in a social world which demands pervasive imitation, role playing, performances, even as it insists on genuineness as a mark of virtue, making it often impossible to tell the difference, even from the first-person point of view.

The funeral scene will amount to nearly our last and certainly most spectacular instance of Sirkian irony, and it ended up more complex than he apparently intended. The overwhelming visual expression is excess, a massive church, a huge white casket covered in flowers, hundreds of mourners, a marching band, a procession, four white horses, an ornate carriage, a display of pomp, flowers and every possible instance of funeral regalia. It is not subtle. (Image 4.13)

Sirk wants us to feel the pathos of someone whose life has been such that the greatest moment of joy and transcendence in it is a moment she cannot enjoy except by anticipation, her official leaving of this life. We recall Annie's last words as Lora tells her that she will not let her go: 'I'm just tired, Miss Lora. Awfully tired.' The film measures by the excess of the lavish display celebrating Annie's leaving, the real if so often hidden misery of the life she lived and is now escaping. The scene is dominated by an extraordinary

Image 4.13

Image 4.14

performance of the hymn 'Trouble of the World' sung by Mahalia Jackson. (Image 4.14)

The lyrics express joy that one is leaving the troubles of this world and is going home to God, and that there will be no more weeping and wailing at the home of God. It is interesting that Jackson (most likely Sirk) leaves out the last stanza of the song, which expresses a further joy, that one will also see one's mother when one lives with God. The reasons are not clear and Sirk never mentions it in his interviews. It is a very famous hymn and the sadness of the last verse would be well known. It could be a comment on Sarah Jane's desertion of and rejection of her mother. In their last scene together, Sarah Jane made it clear that the last thing *she* would *ever* want is to see is her mother again. (She tells her that if they meet on the street she should not show she recognizes her.) It also is a faint reminder that Sarah Jane is not at the funeral, and we could be excused for suspecting at this point that she does not want, yet again, her mother to spoil her attempt at passing as white (although she will appear soon), as well as the very sad fact that Annie, for whom her standing as a mother is the most important in her life, died unacknowledged as such by the most important person in her life, her daughter.

But the power of Jackson's singing almost blows apart Sirk's irony, transforming the ironic excess and pitiable sadness of such a celebration at escape from this life into genuine joy at Annie's divine reward with God.[13] But when the singing stops and we move outside, the level of pomp and excess, almost unimaginably, goes up a few notches and the irony settles back in; a parade, white horses, just as Annie described. The intensity of the melodrama does too as Sarah Jane (whom Steve has apparently found and informed of Annie's death) breaks through the crowd and tearfully embraces the coffin, saying she 'didn't mean it', she did love her mother, is sorry, and she

---

[13]For Sirk's remarks about how surprising he found it that the funeral scene turned out to be so unironically emotional for viewers, see Harvey, 'Sirkumstantial', p. 55.

Image 4.15

believes she 'killed her mother'. Her emotional pain at her mother's death is exponentially intensified by the fact that this is all too little too late, as we remember the lifetime of rejection Annie had to endure.

The funeral scene is nearly our last moment of irony because there is a final and telling, even bitter moment, with Steve and Susie and Lora and now Sarah Jane in a car as part of the procession. Lora, acting the part of the regal matriarch, still as clueless as ever, not at all shaken to discover the vast extent of Annie's status in the black community, still as smug and self-satisfied as ever; as are Steve and Susie. As Lora draws Sarah Jane to her and hugs her, it is as if, again with bitter irony, Sarah Jane has succeeded. Her mother, the mark of her race, is gone and she is now being welcomed into the white world where she will now be able to live, comfortably and safely. Nothing in either world looks like it will change. All that has happened is that Sarah Jane has escaped. (Image 4.15)

Image 4.16

The film ends with the same wall of costume jewellery beads as in the opening credits, reminding us again of how much is obscured in what we see, and how much of that obscurity is due to what we want to avoid seeing, cannot afford to allow ourselves to see. (Image 4.16)

Concluding Remarks

One of the most prominent aesthetic qualities of realist narrative films, often commented on, is that they can possess an immediate, powerful emotional punch. They thereby effortlessly involve us, generate concern for what happens, for the characters; we are terrified of what might happen, relieved when disaster is avoided, puzzled by surprise turns, all even though that cinematic world is both fictional and closed to us (it is present to us, we are never present to or in it). All of the arts of course have emotional power, but films, even, remarkably, badly made or simplistic films, seem to be able to be immediately convincing, *credible*. Whether this is due to the unique features of a photographic art, automatically recording what is real, rather than representing it, or whether we immediately understand that we are to play a 'make believe' game with the filmmaker and so allow ourselves emotional reactions we know are not action-involving,[1] or whether the

---

[1] My own view is that all of these explanations are implausible, but this one seems to me the least plausible explanation, since we do not experience 'make believe' emotions. On the general issue I am in sympathy with D. Rodowick's 'culturalist' agenda, that we need 'a philosophy of the humanities critically and reflexively attentive in equal measure to its epistemological and ethical commitments.' See 'An Elegy for Theory', *October* 122 (Fall 2007): 91–109, and as expressed in the essays collected in *Elegy for Theory* (Cambridge: Harvard University Press, 2014).

sequencing of scenes and dialogue automatically engages the cognitive machinery at work in everyday life in understanding events and actions, this powerful credibility seems to be one of the main reasons people care so much about film, why everyone feels they are entitled to a view of the movies, why they are not intimidated by film, even at its most complex.

The two philosophers most associated with a philosophical appreciation of film, Gilles Deleuze and Stanley Cavell, rely heavily on this feature. They understand film as potentially responding to a crisis – for both a historical crisis – in any confidence we might have in various aspects of the intelligibility of the experienced external and social world. If this were true, it would be hard to deny that this situation certainly poses a 'philosophical problem'. But it is quite an unusual problem: how could it be that 'we' in such a sweeping sense could be said to 'lose confidence' in such a sweeping sense, or that 'we' have come to feel haunted by sceptical doubts as a landmark feature of the modern world, and what would it mean to suggest that film could help us regain a 'belief in the world'? Since the problem cannot be said to be generated (at this level of collectivity and generality) by some discursive argument, it cannot be addressed by such a discursive argument. Even if that were conceivable, how could such a 'case' ever make it out of academe? In such a situation, perhaps it could begin to seem plausible that cinema, a mass art, Hollywood cinema especially, might be able to 'confront' us with the problem; that, say, Italian neo-realism might be able to show us a disordered, highly contingent, purposeless, undirectable world and in a way that did not at all seem exotic, was disturbing, surprising just by being so familiar. And how could our awareness that the film has been able to help us experience and understand that situation be reassuring? For Deleuze this crisis (in his technical terms, the crisis of the action-image)[2] has especially to do with the trauma of the Second World War and a growing sense that our agential powers to transform the world in the service of some idea of the good, or even to control our own destinies, are far weaker than we would like to admit.[3] For Cavell, the historical frame of reference is much broader, post-Cartesian modernity, a subjectivist or representationalist model that forever renders what one might claim about the world or about a fellow human being deeply and permanently dubious. In this context both thinkers can be said to have portrayed cinema as potentially *restorative*, not by showing us how everything can be put right, that things can be made to make perfect sense again, but by showing us ourselves as we are, that we can come to understand *that* difficulty and why it is a difficulty now, and that this situation can be borne, that it is not a problem to be solved, but something like the human condition now. It could then be said to be redeemed by our awareness that it is as it is, by a re-enchantment of the ordinary that had been disenchanted by the modern scientific/sceptical turn, and so be realizing that there is no problem to be fixed, but to be lived out.[4] We can be shown that intelligibility can be better understood as a kind of practical answerability to the world and others, that knowing each other is a matter of acknowledging each other as in the same condition, not by entering each's other minds.

---

[2]Or, more broadly a shift from movement- to time-image cinema.

[3]G. Deleuze, *Cinema I: The Movement Image*, trans. H. Tomlinson and R. Galatea (Minneapolis: The University of Minnesota Press, 1986), pp. 205–07. The neo-realism example is Deleuze's.

[4]S. Cavell, *The World Viewed: Reflections on the Ontology of Film* (Cambridge: Harvard University Press, 1979), p. 21ff, 73.

Both approaches would require considerably more exposition to be presented as the sophisticated views they are, and not the superficial *Weltschmerz* they can seem in such crude summaries.[5] I risk such crudeness for the sake of a final contrast. If the interpretations presented here are convincing, then Sirk's melodramas are disruptive, not restorative in the above sense. Of course, all his films rely on this cinematic, deeply involving believability, and, as it is said, 'work at that level'. There is a clear, compelling, melodramatic narrative line in each film. There is the hyper-emotionality, extreme musical intensification of this emotionality and crises in romantic and familial love typical of melodramas. But as argued above, that excess is put to a distinct ironic use in the sub-genre of subversive melodramas described in the first chapter. The excess creates a tonality that is at once intensifying and distancing.

That is, Sirk's premise is not that this 'crisis analysis' is mistaken, that it is not the case that such confidence has been lost, that it is not the case that mutual intelligibility is now threatened. It is that both we, the viewers, and the characters in the films, are blind, wilfully blind, to this situation, that we don't allow ourselves to see the misrecognition, self-deceit, wishful thinking and our own self-opacity because we can't afford to recognize it, that we are instead smugly complacent, self-deceptively satisfied, that we accept in the film, and in our own lives settle for, the appearance of a form of engagement with each other that is far different than what the engagement actually involves. We, as well as the characters in the three films we have

---

[5]For a more expansive and quite clear summary of these issue, see the account in R. Sinnebrink, *New Philosophies of Film: Thinking Images* (New York: Continuum, 2011), Chapter Five, pp. 90–116.

discussed, actually live in a fantasy world, not the disenchanted one Sirk's films also give us some view of. This all complicates greatly one of the elements of Cavell's linking film to a way of working out, dealing with, scepticism. That the world or a 'projected world' can be present to us without our being present to it can on the one hand intensify a feeling of privacy and anonymity, and on the other undermine our sceptical assumption about the unavailability of the world itself, its availability only as inflected by our viewing it, and so our inability to know the world of others. The cinematic experience can help us overcome these doubts. But Sirk's 'world' cannot be said to be projected to an absent viewer like this; its mode of projection already takes account of the viewer and anticipates a certain sort of blindness and refusal, and thereby challenges the neutrality of the notion of presence.[6] That is, if there is a difference between the 'world of the work', the filmic (Sirkian) world, and the world in the work, the world the characters exist in, then Sirk complicates matters by showing the viewer that the latter world is also a world-viewed, or a world-projected, fantasized within, and the selectivity and directed focus of the filmic world shows us that dimension, not in any directly present way, of the world.[7]

---

[6]Cavell, *The World Viewed*, pp. 40–1. Of course, Cavell concedes that as the period of classic Hollywood ends, traditional ways of understanding the significance of movies 'exemplified by familiar Hollywood cycles and plots that justify the projection of types – are drawing to an end'. He goes on to say that this means 'that they no longer naturally establish conviction in our presentness to the world'. (60) Meta-melodramatic moments like Sirk (and there were plenty in the 1930s and 1940s too) do not reflect anything 'coming to an end' as much as an attempt to end the ideal of a presentness of a world now so distorted, blind to itself and manipulated as to make its implied relation to the viewer much more complicated.

[7]Cf. the discussion of this issue in D. Yacavone, *Film Worlds: A Philosophic Aesthetics of Cinema* (New York: Columbia University Press, 2015), pp. 3, 26, 29, 31.

Hence the kind of reversal or second thoughts typical of Sirk's films. In *All That Heaven Allows* we see, involve ourselves in, care about, a narrative of what appears to be wavering but finally heroic resistance to stupid social conformism, but on a second or a third viewing, Ron's smirk, the strangeness of his 'be a man' advice, Cary's not knocking at Ron's cabin, refusing reconciliation, the décor of the house they have ended up in, the role of the doctor, the deadness and passionless calm in the final scene, all make that affirmation begin to seem hasty, and we feel if not exactly ashamed, at least chastened and somewhat confused, perhaps even more mistrustful. We have had too much trust, faith, in the world being as we ordinarily take it in, too much faith in the ordinary itself. We have not lost faith in the world's intelligibility; we are not burdened by powerful sceptical doubts. We should have, should be, but the *problem* is: we are not. Sirk is aware that the very popularity of his melodramas is built on this blindness. So we at first are relieved that the selfish brats in *Written on the Wind* do not win the Hadley game, and the responsible, square good guys will ride off together, but we remember the loneliness and pain of the siblings, the coldness of Lucy, the bitterness of the false friend Mitch, the opportunism of both, and our faith in our own and their moralism is shaken. We are relieved that Sarah Jane has finally admitted to herself her need for her mother and her love for her, then we realize she is finally only able to say all this to a corpse, that Lora is as smugly ignorant and self-satisfied as ever, that Sarah Jane's attempt at passing has now solved its biggest problem, her mother's presence and love for her, that the grandeur of Annie's funeral is a measure of the misery of her life.

There is no reason to think that Sirk has any confidence that the possibility of such emotional reversals, reassessments and appreciation for irony are signs that the power of middle-class conformism, smug moralism and an evasive blindness about race and inauthentic posing can all be challenged. His films are suffused with quite a pessimistic fatalism about these aspects of the bourgeois world, even as he also manages to express a deep, humane sympathy for those caught in the grip of such social forces. The need for a protective blindness and for projecting fantasies are as powerfully credible in his films as is the equally credible display of the destructiveness of such a need.

BIBLIOGRAPHY

Brooks, P. *The Melodramatic Imagination: Balzac, Henry James, Melodrama and the Mode of Excess* (New Haven: Yale University Press, 1976).

Camper, F. 'The Films of Douglas Sirk', in *Screen*, 12 (2) (1971).

Cavell, S. *The World Viewed: Reflections on the Ontology of Film* (Cambridge: Harvard University Press, 1979).

Cavell, S. *The Pursuits of Happiness. The Hollywood Comedy of Remarriage* (Cambridge: Harvard University Press, 1981).

Cavell, S. 'Politics as Opposed to What', in *Critical Inquiry*, 9 (September 1982).

Cavell, S. *This New Yet Unapproachable America* and *Conditions Handsome and Unhandsome: The Constitution of Emersonian Perfectionism* (Chicago: University of Chicago Press, 1991).

Cavell, S. *Contesting Tears: The Hollywood melodrama of the Unknown Woman* (Chicago: University of Chicago Press, 1997).

Cavell, S. *The Claim of Reason: Wittgenstein, Skepticism, Morality, and Tragedy* (Oxford: Oxford University Press, 1999).

Coates, P. *The Gorgon's Gaze: German Cinema, Expressionism, and the Image of Horror* (New York: Cambridge University Press).

Comolli, J.-L. and P. Narboli, 'Cinema/Ideology/Criticism', reprinted from *Cahiers du Cinéma* in *Screen*, 12 (1) (1971).

Conroy, M. '"No sin in lookin' prosperous": Gender, Race and the Class Formations of Middlebrow Taste in Douglas Sirk's *Imitation of Life*', in James and Berg 1996.

Deleuze, G. *Cinema I: The Movement Image*, trans. H. Tomlinson and R. Galatea (Minneapolis: The University of Minnesota Press, 1986).

Elsaesser, T. 'Tales of Sound and Fury: Observations on the Family Melodrama', first published in *Monogram* in 1972, and reprinted in Gledhill 1994.

Evans, P.W. *Written on the Wind* (London: Palgrave McMillan, 2013).

Fassbinder, R. 'Six Films by Douglas Sirk', in L. Mulvey and J. Halliday, *Douglas Sirk* (Edinburgh: Edinburgh Film Festival, 1972).

Fassbinder, R. *The Anarchy of the Imagination: Interviews, Essays, Notes* (Baltimore: Johns Hopkins University Press, 1992).

Fischer, L. 'Three-Way Mirror: *Imitation of Life*', in Fischer, L. ed. *Imitation of Life: Douglas Sirk, Director* (New Brunswick: Rutgers University Press, 1991).

Girard, R. *Deceit, Desire, and the Novel: Self and Other in Literary Structure*, transl. Y. Freccero (Baltimore: The Johns Hopkins University Press, 1961).

Gledhill, 'The Melodramatic Field: An Investigation', in Gledhill 1994.

Halliday, J. ed. *Sirk on Sirk: Conversations with Jon Halliday* (London: Faber and Faber, 1971).

Harvey, J. 'Sirkumstanial Evidence', in *Film Comment* 14, no. 4 (1978).

Harvey, J. *Movie Love in the Fifties* (Cambridge: Da Capo Press, 2001).

Heilman, R. *Tragedy and Melodrama* (Seattle and London: University of Washington Press, 1968).

James, C. and Berg, R. eds. *The Hidden Foundation: Cinema and the Question of Class* (Minneapolis: University of Minnesota Press, 1996).

Kaplan, A.E. 'The Case of the Missing Mother: Maternal Issues in Vidor's *Stella Dallas*', in Kaplan 2000.

Kaplan, A.E. ed. *Feminism and Film* (Oxford: Oxford University Press, 2000).

Klinger, B. 'Much ado about Excess: Genre, Mise-en-Scene and the Woman in *Witten on the Wind*', *Wide Angle*, 11.4 (1989).

Klinger, B. *Melodrama and Meaning: History, Culture, and the Films of Douglas Sirk* (Bloomington, Ind., 1994).

MacDowell, J. *Happy Endings in Hollywood Cinema: Cliché, Convention and the Happy Couple* (Edinburgh: University of Edinburgh Press, 2013).

MacDowell, J. 'Interpretation, Irony, and "Surface Meanings" in Film', in *Film-Philosophy* 22, no. 2 (2018).

MacDowell, J. *Irony in Film* (London, 2016).

Mercer, J. and Shingler, M. *Melodrama: Genre, Style, Sensibility* (London: Wallflower, 2004).

Mulvey, L. 'Notes on Sirk and Melodrama', in Gledhill 1994.

Nietzsche, F. *Die fröhliche Wissenschaft*, in *Sämtliche Werke*. Studien Ausgabe. Bd. 3. Ed. G. Colli and M. Montinari (Berlin: de Gruyter, 1988).

Nietzsche, F. *The Gay Science*, ed. B. Williams, J. Nauckhoff and transl. A. Del Caro (Cambridge: Cambridge University Press, 2001).

Orr, C. 'Closure and Containment: Marylee Hadley in *Written on the Wind*', in *Wide Angle*, 4.2 (1980).

Pippin, R. *Hollywood Westerns and American Myth: The Importance of Howard Hawks and John Ford for Political Philosophy* (New Haven: Yale University Press, 2010).

Pippin, R. *Fatalism in American Film Noir: Some Cinematic Philosophy* (Charlottesville: University of Virginia Press, 2012).

Pippin, R. *The Philosophical Hitchcock: Vertigo and the Anxieties of Unknowingness* (Chicago: University of Chicago Press, October 2017).

Pippin, R. *Filmed Thought. Cinema as Reflective Form* (Chicago: University of Chicago Press, 1919).

Rasner, H.-G. and Wulf, R. 'An Encounter with Douglas Sirk', transl. V. Soukup, in *Filmkritik*, no. 203 (Nov. 2002).

Rodowick, D.N. 'Madness, Authority and ideology: The Domestic Melodrama of the 1950s', in Gledhill 1994.

Rodowick, D. 'An Elegy for Theory', in *October*, 122 (Fall 2007).

Rodowick, D. *Elegy for Theory* (Cambridge: Harvard University Press, 2014).

Rushton, R. 'Douglas Sirk's Theatres of Imitation', in *Screening the Past*, Issue 21 (2007).

Ryan, T. *The Films of Douglas Sirk: Exquisite Ironies and Magnificent Obsessions* (Jackson: University Press of Mississippi, 2019).

Schatz, T. 'Douglas Sirk and the Family Melodrama: Hollywood Baroque', in Schatz, T. *Hollywood Genres: Formulas. Filmmaking and the Studio System* (New York: Random House, 1981).

Segond, J. 'The Bad and the Beautiful: sur Stella Dallas et le wedding night', in *Positif*, no. 163 (Nov. 1974).

Selig, M. 'Contradiction and Reading: Social Class and Sex Class in *Imitation of Life*', in *Wide Angle*, 10.4 (1988).

Sinnebrink, R. *New Philosophies of Film: Thinking Images* (New York: Continuum, 2011).

Stern, M. 'Patterns of Power and Potency, Repression and Violence: An Introduction to the Films of Douglas Sirk', in *The Velvet Light Trap*, no. 16 (Fall 1976).

Stern, M. *Douglas Sirk* (Boston: Twain Publishers, 1979).

Töteberg, M. and L. Lensing, L. eds. *The Anarchy of the Imagination: Interviews, Essays, Notes. Rainer Werner Fassbinder* (Baltimore: Johns Hopkins University Press, 1992).

Trilling, L. *Sincerity and Authenticity* (Cambridge: Harvard University Press, 1973).

Wegner, H. 'Melodrama as Tragic Rondo – Douglas Sirk's *Written on the Wind*', in *Literature/Film Quarterly* 10.3 (1982).

Willemen, P. 'Distanciation and Douglas Sirk', in *Screen*, 12 (2) (1971).

Yacavone, D. *Film Worlds: A Philosophic Aesthetics of Cinema* (New York: Columbia University Press, 2015).

INDEX